Mindfulness Techniques

Created Through Spiritual Mindfulness and Meditation, Peace and Happiness

(How to Stop Worrying, Find Inner Peace and Live a Depression Free Life With Mindfulness and Meditation)

Richard Copeland

Published by Rob Miles

© **Richard Copeland**

All Rights Reserved

Mindfulness Techniques: Created Through Spiritual Mindfulness and Meditation, Peace and Happiness (How to Stop Worrying, Find Inner Peace and Live a Depression Free Life With Mindfulness and Meditation)

ISBN 978-1-990084-01-0

All rights reserved. No part of this guide may be reproduced in any form without permission in writing from the publisher except in the case of brief quotations embodied in critical articles or reviews.

LEGAL & DISCLAIMER

The information contained in this book is not designed to replace or take the place of any form of medicine or professional medical advice. The information in this book has been provided for educational and entertainment purposes only.

The information contained in this book has been compiled from sources deemed reliable, and it is accurate to the best of the Author's knowledge; however, the Author cannot guarantee its accuracy and validity and cannot be held liable for any errors or omissions. Changes are periodically made to this book. You must consult your doctor or get professional medical advice before using any of the suggested remedies, techniques, or information in this book.

Upon using the information contained in this book, you agree to hold harmless the Author from and against any damages, costs, and expenses, including any legal fees potentially resulting from the application of any of the information provided by this guide. This disclaimer applies to any damages or injury caused by the use and application, whether directly or indirectly, of any advice or information presented, whether for breach of contract, tort, negligence, personal injury, criminal intent, or under any other cause of action.

You agree to accept all risks of using the information presented inside this book. You need to consult a professional medical practitioner in order to ensure you are both able and healthy enough to participate in this program.

Table of Contents

INTRODUCTION 1

CHAPTER 1: PREPARATION: SETTING AND BODY MECHANICS 4

CHAPTER 2: KNOW YOUR STRESSORS 11

CHAPTER 3: COUPLES EXERCISE 15

CHAPTER 4: FREEING YOURSELF FROM WORRY 18

CHAPTER 5: LEARNING TO CULTIVATE HAPPINESS 24

CHAPTER 6: THE PATH TO MINDFULNESS 34

CHAPTER 7: HOW TO LIVE STRESS-FREE AND IN THE MOMENT 38

CHAPTER 8: MINDFUL BEHAVIOR 48

CHAPTER 9: PRACTICE MINDFUL BREATHING□ 53

CHAPTER 10: WHERE TO PRACTICE MINDFULNESS? 58

CHAPTER 11: CONTROL SHYNESS AND SOCIAL ANXIETY .. 63

CHAPTER 12: PREPARING FOR MINDFULNESS 74

CHAPTER 13: THE MINDFULNESS EXPERIENCE 80

CHAPTER 14: MINDFULNESS IN MANAGING YOUR LIFE ... 90

CHAPTER 15: THE TOP TEN TIPS FOR BEING MINDFUL 95

CHAPTER 16: MINDFULNESS IN EVERYDAY LIFE 101

CHAPTER 17: MINDFULNESS FOR PHYSICAL TROUBLES . 107

- CHAPTER 18: THE POWER OF BREATHING 113
- CHAPTER 19: MENTAL ILLNESS☐ 116
- CHAPTER 20: MINDFULNESS IN EVERYDAY LIFE 121
- CHAPTER 21: FIND FOCUS AND TUNE INTO THE HERE AND NOW 128
- CHAPTER 22: BREATHING EXERCISES TECHNIQUE 134
- CHAPTER 23: MINDFULNESS AND DISTRACTIONS 138
- CHAPTER 24: TIPS TO TAKE IT ALL THE WAY 151
- CHAPTER 25: BEGINNER'S GUIDE TO MINDFULNESS 156
- CHAPTER 26: WHY IS AWARENESS SO IMPORTANT? 160
- CHAPTER 27: THE SENSE OF TOUCH 170
- CHAPTER 28: HOW TO PRACTICE MINDFULNESS TO ENSURE BEST POSSIBLE RESULTS 175
- CHAPTER 29: LETTING GO OF NEGATIVITY 178
- CHAPTER 28: HOW TO MEDITATE FOR STRESS RELIEF ... 182
- CHAPTER 29: MINDFULNESS FOR WORKING PROFESSIONAL 188
- CONCLUSION 192

Introduction

Are you finding it hard to relax? Do you always feel stressed and exhausted? Do you feel like life is just flying by? If you do, then you're one of many. Unending stress and feeling like you're just constantly racing against the clock can take a toll on your physical, mental and emotional health. These are all modern day problems, but you can look to the past for a solution.

Meditation is a practice that has been in existence since antiquity and the positive benefits have stood the test of time. Meditation and mindfulness have proven effective in combatting depression and chronic pain, and it can certainly do wonders to help you deal with day-to-day stress.

This book will show you:

- How to find out the causes of stress in your life and how meditation can change those;

- How taking a little time for yourself every day can guide you to your true nature and change your entire outlook;

- How to create strong foundations for your practice, such as the correct attitude and intentions that you should foster;

- How to gain confidence, develop self-discipline, and strengthen concentration and focus through meditation;

- And, finally, clear, simple, step-by-step guides on simple to intermediate techniques that can help you start your practice and deepen it, along with some tips on how to develop the perfect practice.

Meditation is a very simple practice that won't cost you much. All you really have to spend is time and effort in building your practice. This is a small price to pay for such life-changing benefits. Through meditation, you can learn self-love, powers of concentration, inner peace, goodwill to all, and an unshakable sense of happiness.

Meditation can empower you to experience life in the best way possible and savor every aspect of life with positivity and loving-kindness. So what are waiting for? Grab this book and delve into the wonderful possibilities of meditation!

Chapter 1: Preparation: Setting And Body Mechanics

The practice of meditation entails establishing a formal schedule specifically devoted to cultivating mindfulness. This is not an easy task. Developing mental habits require energy. This may seem quite counterproductive to the idea of meditation, which should be free flowing and natural. To address this, a bit of strategy is needed. Since the mind is like a cup of muddy water, allow a specific time to clarify it first. At the start of your meditation practice, give your mind enough time to settle down so you wind up with clear water. Do not do anything to force this settling as it should be a natural, spontaneous process. The very act of sitting down leads to mind settling.

Where to Sit

The condition of your surroundings affect your meditative practice. Choose a place that is quiet and uplifts you even if it only is a tiny corner of your apartment. It should be away from too much noise (though not necessarily sound-proof) and other stimuli, or a place where your emotions cannot easily be provoked. It may be helpful to sit in the same spot solely reserved for meditation. You will soon associate this place with the serenity of deep concentration, helping you reach deep states faster.

Certain traditional paraphernalia can help you set the proper mood. You can darken the room and light a candle or incense. You can also ring a little bell to signal the start and end of your sessions. They may be encouragement to some; however, they are by no means crucial to the meditation practice.

When to Sit

The Middle Ways, as a description of Buddhism, is considered as a rule in setting a time for your mindfulness meditation: Do not underdo it. Do not overdo it. Set up a practice schedule and stick to it. Remember that your schedule should feel like an encouragement and not a burden.

It is good to meditate in the morning when your mind is fresh, before getting yourself buried in your daily responsibilities. This tunes you up and lets you handle things throughout the day more efficiently. Take note that you should be completely awake. Wash your face or take a shower before starting. You may first do a bit of exercise to get your circulation flowing. Meditating in the evening is also fine. It is a great way to cleanse and rejuvenate your mind of all the burdens that have accumulated during the day. It also helps you sleep better.

For beginners, meditating once a day is enough. It is fine if you feel like you want to meditate more, just remember not to overdo it. Allot time to integrate meditation into your life, and let the practice grow gradually. Make it a steady and consistent effort. As you become more interested in meditation, you will find yourself making more room for it in your schedule. For some seasoned meditators, three to four hours of practice comes naturally without making any negative impact in their daily lives.

How to Sit

The Buddhist approach to meditation follows that body and mind should be connected. There is better energy flow throughout the body if it is positioned erectly. Bending the body changes the flow, which can directly interrupt your thought process. If you need a chair to do meditation, sit up straight with feet planted on the ground. If you prefer using a cushion such as a gomden or zafu, sit comfortably with legs crossed and your hands placed on your thighs palm-down. The hips should not be rotated forward nor tilted back. You must have a feeling of strength and stability. Your shoulders should be leveled as well as your hips. Your spine should be straight and aligned.

The first thing you must have is body awareness. You may prop yourself up on a chair and yet not be completely attuned to what your body is actually feeling. When starting a meditation session, spend some time settling into your posture. Feel how your spine is being drawn up from the top of your head in a way that your posture is lengthened. You can imagine placing your bones in the right order and your flesh hanging off that structure. This will help you feel relaxed and very much awake. Check and correct your posture at once if you find yourself getting hazy, dull, or falling asleep.

For strict mindfulness practice, open your eyes and gaze downwards, softly focusing two inches in front of your nose. This will make you purposefully ignore what is going on in the surroundings, reducing sensory input as much as possible.

How Long To Sit

Sit as long as you can, but, again, do not overdo it. Most beginners meditate for twenty or thirty minutes. It may initially be difficult to sit longer than this. Since the posture and mental skills are generally unfamiliar to Westerners, it will take some time for their body to adjust to them. As you become accustomed to the practice, you can extend your sessions gradually. It is recommended that after around one year of steady practice, you should be meditating comfortably for one hour per session.

As a general rule, determine the minimum length of time that is comfortable for you to practice then add five more minutes to it. There is, however, no strict rule as to the duration for sitting. There would be days when it will be physically impossible for you to sit longer (e.g. due to illness). This does not mean cancelling your meditation for the day though, as it is crucial to meditate regularly. Ten minutes of practice is already very beneficial.

Take note that you should decide the duration of your session before starting, and not while meditating. This will easily predispose you to restlessness. You can use a watch but you should not look at it every several minutes to see how you are doing. This completely kills your concentration, and agitation will set in. Do not peek at the clock until you think the whole meditation period has passed. Ideally, you do not even have to consult the clock at all, or at least not during every session.

Chapter 2: Know Your Stressors

If we want to win the battle against depression, stress, and anxiety in order to experience life to the fullest, it's important to know what you're up against. Specifically, we need to know what stressors are in order to overcome them. Here are the most common stressors that we may not be aware of but are experiencing regularly:

☐ Insufficient Time: One of the most powerful stressors that we can encounter, which can make us extremely stressed and anxious, is trying to finish very important and urgent things with so little time. If this is our normal daily situation, chances are that we'll suffer from very high stress levels. And guess what? Excessive chronic stress has been scientifically connected to many serious diseases or sicknesses, which can be fatal.

☐ So Many Things To Do: This particular stressor is similar to having insufficient time in the sense that it can make us feel so overwhelmed and eventually lead to chronic stress or worse, getting sick. Many times, it's not a matter of having enough time but simply about taking on too many things.

☐ Bad Habits: Such habits include excessive consumption of alcohol, a sedentary lifestyle, a diet composed mainly of processed and junk foods, overheating, and smoking, among others. Such habits may seem to provide much relief and comfort during stressful moments but to the contrary, they can actually stress us out even more and make us feel more anxious, even depressed.

How's that? It's because Habits like these tend to result in very poor health or serious sicknesses. And we all know that sicknesses and diseases – more often than not – makes us more stressed, anxious, or depressed. Thus begins the crazy cycle of stress-sickness-stress-sickness.

☐ Insufficient Rest And Recreation: One of the important things in life that is often taken for granted is rest or sleep. The thing is, chronic lack of such is one of the most stressful things we can ever experience in our lives.

When we don't get enough sleep or rest, it's highly unlikely we'll be able to recover well from the day before, especially if it was a stressful one. As such, it's highly likely that we will lack the energy, the job, even desire to do well the next day. Feeling this way can be very stressful, especially if we have to finish a lot of things. When this becomes the norm for us, we can expect our stress levels to either touch the roof or go through it. And we all know what happens after that.

☐ Improbable Expectations: If you would like to be consistently disappointed, anxious, best, or even depressed, the best thing you can do is to set for yourself - and others - expectations that are very improbable to meet. How does this work?

Improbable expectations have a consistent track record of keeping people from accomplishing them. When we set improbable expectations, we are setting ourselves up for consistent failures. And obviously, this can be very stressful.

Win The Battle

The stressors that we identified above can't be managed well or overcome, which can get in the way of us experiencing life to the phone, if we simply go with the flow or let things be. If we don't take charge over our stressors, they will take charge of us.

As such, we shouldn't live mindlessly or on autopilot but instead, live with awareness and purpose. By practicing the art of mindfulness, we can experience how the challenges and busyness of life lose their grips on us and as well as minimize their power to make us anxious, or even depressed. And when this happens, we can start living our lives to the full.

Chapter 3: Couples Exercise

This is a mindfulness exercise for couples that will help to increase intimacy.

Sometimes you grow closer to your partner when you are away from them. In this exercise, you will do just that. One of you can read the instructions during the exercise or you can have someone read them for you.

To begin this mindfulness exercise for couples, stand back-to-back in the center of the room. Simply stand there with your backs touching.

Breathe. Notice how it feels like to stand back to back with your partner. Notice what thoughts arise within you.

After a few minutes of standing back-to-back, both partners take one step away from each other. Stand in this new place for one minute and notice what you feel. Examine how you feel in your body. Notice any changes for you in this new position. Pay specific attention to your back that was touching your partner's back previously. Simply accept what you are feeling in your body in this moment.

After a mindful pause in this new position, repeat this step three more times. After each pause, you'll move one step further away from your partner and likewise for your partner. In each new spot, pause to notice what is going on inside of you. Any thoughts? Any sensations? Any memories?

Following these four mindful steps and pauses away from your partner, turn and face each other. Notice if anything chages within you when you turn to face your partner. Notice what arises.

After a mindful pause while facing one another, take one step toward each other and be aware of what is happening in your body as you do that. Pause to feel and acknowledge it. Remember that whatever arises within you during this exercise is ok.

Repeat these mindful steps and pause toward your partner until the two of you are standing nose to nose. Notice what you feel in your body. Remember that all feelings, emotions, and sensations are welcome. Pause to feel them and acknowledge them. Notice how it feels like to stand so close to your partner.

After this exercise, you and your partner might want to take a few minutes to note down some of your personal responses to this exercise. Freeform writing works well to capture the feelings, emotions, and sensations that arose. Others may prefer to draw something that arose for them. Do what feels right for you.

Chapter 4: Freeing Yourself From Worry

Mindfulness originally started with Buddhism. However, even those who are not religious can benefit from adding it to their daily lives and benefiting. Famous author and meditation instructor Jon Kabat-Zinn says that mindfulness means deciding to pay attention to the present without judging it. Many people are too aware of the thoughts going on inside their minds and wish that they could get less caught up in this. It is often the case that people see life through a habitual, biased filter full of fear, criticism, and a lack of patience.

Mindfulness Method Number Five: Use it to Lessen Worry.

Someone who has been depressed before might react strongly even when they experience a small mood fluctuation. This might cause them to shift into thinking negatively and feeling depressed. For example, someone who has been depressed before might worry all the time that they are going to retreat back into it. They might feel sad and analyze themselves, trying to find answers for why they feel the way they feel. Although this appears a logical way to approach the problem, it only adds to the feelings of sadness in most people. During this therapy, the clients are instructed to notice and challenge any errors they see in the way they think.

Observing Thoughts: You can learn from these techniques by starting to observe your own negative thoughts and ideas. Instead of fighting or resisting them, which only creates more judgment and tension, try to just accept that they are thoughts and do not hold any power over you unless you let them. You do not have to give them so much energy and focus. During mindfulness therapy, patients learn how to gradually take their negative feelings and thoughts less seriously, and instead react to them in different ways, thus earning back their personal power and strength.

Shifting your Focus to Bodily Sensations: By learning how to recognize when you are analyzing and judging, you can start to be mindful and happier in your life. What feelings come along with the activity of analyzing? Which sensations are in your body when you start to analyze your life or get very distracted mentally? Keeping a curious, friendly, and open awareness to these sensations can help you with acceptance toward the moment. You can then choose which way you will engage instead of unconsciously fulfilling the same old reactions as you usually do. Perhaps you can do some writing to get your feelings out or go exercise to get rid of that excess nervous energy you are feeling.

People make all sorts of excuses for not paying attention more in their lives. Perhaps they think that they do not have time to meditate or even to pay attention to their life situation. Even those who want to make meditation a part of their lives make up excuses constantly, or even forget to do it. They might start the practice and then give up after one week because it is "too hard" to focus on and stick with. These are the most common excuses or obstacles that people report when trying to be more mindful. So how are you to overcome these difficulties and stick with the path that you know is good for you?

Mindfulness Method Number Six: Get Curious and Creative.

Learning to be more mindful should be the most personal journey you ever go on. This means sitting in a variety of meditation postures, finding creative methods for paying more attention to your breath, and looking at different ways to keep your mind focused when it tries to wander. Let's look at some other keys to becoming curious and creative with your mindfulness practice:

Exploration: Commit to exploring everything that happens as your present moment rises and falls with your breath. Refrain from critical thinking or judgment when possible, but forgive yourself when you do this subconsciously. Anytime you feel distracted by a thought, make sure that you investigate it momentarily and then focus on your breathing again.

Zest for Learning: See your commitment to mindfulness as a chance to constantly learn new things about yourself. You can also pursue mindfulness material to read as a new way to stay mentally engaged with your practice. Then go on walks as a way to blend together mindfulness meditation and activity.

Kindness and Love: Positive feelings such as kindness and love are essential for a mindfulness practice. You might find it helpful to dedicate your meditation sessions to someone you care about that has passed away. As you meditate, remember to feel compassion not just for others, but for yourself as well. Try to have empathy for those who are less fortunate in the world and make that part of your practice as well.

All of these can put you in closer touch with the present moment and make you more mindful throughout your daily existence. But remember that although there are guidelines in this book to follow, you shouldn't hesitate to find your own way and invent methods that help you stay mindful.

Chapter 5: Learning To Cultivate Happiness

In learning the teachings of the Buddha you will find they are based on simple straightforward logic and reasoning nothing complex but just plain and simple. Quite simply if we truly want to end suffering then we need to eliminate the causes of suffering. It also stands to reason that if we truly want happiness then we need to seek ways in which to cultivate its causes.

These teachings were given in hopes that we would truly understand what actually happens to us thus helping us to find ways to change the undesirable things we do and work towards more positive actions in life. According to the Buddha suffering, anxiety and fears come from minds that have become overpowered with distraction and delusion.

But if we can learn to tame our minds then we will fear nothing all fear originates from an untamed mind. Think of the personal feats you will be able to accomplish by taming your mind. But in order for you to be able to tame your mind you first must understand what it is and how it works.

The Most Important Factor is Your Mind. By learning and investigating about your mind and the way it works does not mean

you have to make any drastic changes in

your life or the way that you live.

But it is important that you realize how your mind is the most important factor that is involved with all of your everyday living experiences in life. It is ultimately also responsible for everything you will experience in life. Understanding your mind and the true nature of your thoughts, mental attitudes, and emotions will help you to be more effective in not only helping yourself but others as well. The true nature of the mind is not only thoughts and emotions; these are just the appearance of the mind to most people.

Two Main Aspects of the Mind:

the appearance of the mind

and the nature of the mind

We spend most of our lives looking for ourselves outside of ourselves lost in the appearance of the mind without understanding the mind itself.

We do not understand that "ourselves" have been buried deep within us waiting to be released. A way to help us find ourselves is through the practice of Meditation. We are so busy trying to find ourselves on the outside that we as the saying goes "can't see the trees for the forest." We are so caught up in what is going on outside of us that we have completely lost touch with our inner selves. We get carried away and swept up into the delusions and promises that we have been fed by the outer world that this was the true path to happiness.

We get convinced that by gaining "outer wealth" we will reach true happiness. But many have found this to be an empty promise.

We Have the Potential to Transform. It is how our minds perceive appearances and tries to make them real or solidify them that can be a problem. In Buddhist teachings we are advised to purify the projections of our minds and realize the nature of the mind in understanding life through the eyes of someone who understands how their mind truly works.

It is possible to transform ones way of thinking and viewing the world as the Dalai Lama pointed out: "A great Tibetan teacher of mind training once remarked that one of the mind's most marvellous qualities is that it can be transformed."

Through the continuous use of meditation we will be able to tame our minds by becoming more in tune and familiar with the true essence of the mind. We will become masters of our own perceptions when we conquer our own minds. When we transform our perceptions even the appearances of things will begin to change for us. Once we are through with taming our mind we will be able to arrive at the profound purity of the nature of mind.

This is the great peace that the Buddha spoke of that happened during his enlightenment over 2,500 years ago in India underneath a Bodhi tree in what is known as Bodhgaya. By allowing meditation to be part of your life you are opening the doors to your inner self that you probably have never made a true connection with until you started meditating.

How can we transform our minds using meditation? First of all you cannot force your mind to transform but you should approach your mind in a friendly way showing your mind that you want to build a connection with it by learning about it and how it works.

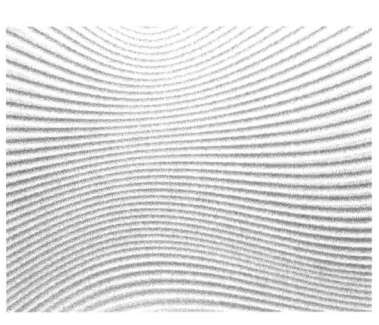

You won't be able to make friends with your mind if you continue to try and block out thoughts or emotions by suppressing them and trying to make them go away. But you do not want your mind to have all the power over you so don't totally surrender yourself to it either. But instead make friends with it by finding out what your mind really loves.

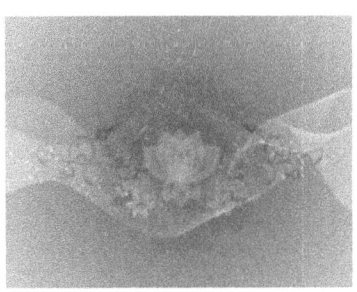

The conceptual mind loves having things to do; it loves nothing more than being active and getting stimulated by new knowledge. It can get into trouble if it is not kept busy. So to start building your friendship with your mind give it the job of meditation. This will be a win-win situation for you and your mind. Your mind is going to be happy with its new job of meditation and you are going to be happy that you are in charge of your own mind. Nobody else but you are your mind's keeper.

You will become free of your conceptual mind no longer being fixated on emotions and thoughts but free and in control of your own mind making choices in your life that will benefit you by helping you in finding peace and contentment in your life.

Chapter 6: The Path To Mindfulness

Preparation and Logistics

Now, the time has come to prepare yourself for the guided meditations. First of all, you will need to make yourself physically comfortable in a safe space in which you can unwind and open yourself to cosmic energies.

Ready your environment. Declutter your surroundings. Create a space that will not distract you from navigating your own spiritual journey. Perhaps light a scented candle or a stick of incense. A soothing aroma may help guide your senses to a more pleasurable frame of mind. A sweet wave of lavender or vanilla may provide you with a calmness otherwise unfounded in your chosen space of meditation. The earthy tones of sandalwood or lemongrass may help lull you into a trance, a state of mind susceptible to spiritual guidance. You may prefer nectarous scents like a mandarin orange or red apple. Let the candle's flame flicker. Let the incense stick pour its smoke.

Perhaps, brew yourself a cup of herbal tea. Establish a connection with nature by ingesting a steeped herb, flower, or root. Allow the sweet, earthy liquid to clear your nasal passages. Unencumbered breathing is integral to meditation. A steaming cup of tea will warm your insides and loosen your muscles by relieving them of unwanted stress. It will help your body sink into your meditation. Let the tea replenish your body with essential antioxidants and vitamins. Tune your body with this natural remedy.

Are you wearing comfortable clothing? It is crucial that what you are wearing does not inhibit your ability to breathe. Loose fitting clothing or breathable fabrics are recommended. Is the temperature of your space to your liking? Will a lack or excess of warmth or cold break your concentration? Adjust your setting. Create a space that's right for you.

Choose a spot to sit or lie down. Do not engage in meditation while engaged in other activities like walking or driving. Your body must be stationary, you must be open and ready to receive spiritual guidance. Allow yourself to concentrate on the journey ahead.

Perhaps you have a favorite chair in which to sit on. A bed, a couch, or a cushioned mat on the floor are also acceptable places to situate yourself for a session of meditation. Fluff your pillows or cushions. Ready your favorite fuzzy blanket. Maybe employ a face mask to black out your surroundings. Allow your body to sink into whatever space you choose.

Distance yourself from polluting noise. It is unideal to allow in loud engines on the road, trains chugging past, loud voices outside your window, rattling footsteps, dogs barking, cats hissing, dump trucks clunking along, or the ringing of a phone. Silence your phone and shut down your computer. Separate yourself from the noise. Use headphones or a loud enough speaker set to listen to the meditations. Submerge yourself in the journey, and eliminate any possible distractions. All five senses must be wholly committed to the journey in order to achieve ultimate relaxation.

In this and the next chapters I would like to share with you my guided meditations which aim to balance your inner energy. The ultimate goal is to help you feel grounded and content. First, I will I guide you into a deep state of relaxation. Then we will continue with Mindfulness meditations.

Chapter 7: How To Live Stress-Free And In The Moment

The tips shared in this chapter can only help you achieve what you are after if you practice them on a daily basis and not have breaks in between. Once you get the hang of it, these tips will automatically become an essential part of your life and your daily routine.

1.Begin little by little. While you may be enticed to totally redesign your way of life, it is not important to roll out huge improvements to begin living at the time. Begin by consolidating new propensities each one in turn. When you have a feeling that you have aced a propensity, include something else.

2.For instance, rather than attempting to contemplate for 20 minutes for each day immediately, begin by attempting to ruminate for three minutes for each day. At that point, expand your time as you turn out to be more OK with reflection.

Stroll to work with your telephone in your pocket. Don't content or chat on the telephone unless it is a crisis.

3.Divert your brain when it meanders. It is typical for your brain to meander, yet with a specific end goal to live at the time, you have to keep your psyche concentrated on the present. When you see that your brain is meandering, use tender redirection to concentrate on the present once more. Recognize that your psyche is meandering without judging yourself for doing as such.

4.Try not to get angry with yourself if your brain meanders. It is ordinary for your psyche to meander here and there. Simply acknowledge that you took somewhat mental excursion and return your center to the present.

5.Pick a care signal. It might be hard to recollect to be careful when you are exceptionally occupied. A care prompt, for example, a string that is tied around your wrist, or a coin in your shoe a pen mark on your hand, can help you to recall to be careful. When you see the signal, ensure that you pause for a minute to stop and notice your environment. You can likewise utilize something more outside like making some tea, looking in the mirror, or evacuating your shoes after work as your sign. Before long, you may start to disregard the sign since you are utilized to it. In the event that this happens, change your signal to something else.

6.Grin and chuckle all the more frequently. Living at the time can be a test on the off chance that you are in a terrible state of mind or simply feeling somewhat down, however grinning and chuckling can improve you feel even you compel yourself to grin and laugh. If you find that you are not centered around the present since you feel troubled, constrain yourself to grin and giggle a bit. Regardless of the fact that you put on a fake grin and giggle foolishly, you ought to begin to feel better immediately.

7.Do kind things for others. Performing irregular demonstrations of benevolence can help you to live at the time by refocusing your consideration on what's going on before you. Search for little things that you can do to show consideration to others. The kind demonstrations that you perform will help you to back off and see your environment.

8.For instance, you could offer a compliment to an outsider. Look for approaches to show consideration in whatever circumstance you are in. Notwithstanding something as straightforward as grinning and gesturing at individuals for the duration of the day may light up somebody's day and keep you concentrated on the present.

9.Do one thing at once. Single-assignment, don't multi-undertaking. When you're pouring water, simply pour water. When you're eating, simply eat. When you're washing, simply bathe. Try not to attempt to knock off a couple assignments while eating or washing or driving. A famous Zen adage: "When walking, walk. Whenever eating, eat."

10. Concentrate on what is currently, quit stressing over what's to come. Turned out to be more mindful of your reasoning - would you say you are continually stressing over what's to come? Figure out how to perceive when you're doing this, and after that work on taking yourself back to the present. Simply concentrate on what you're doing, at this moment. Appreciate the present minute.

11. In the event that something is irritating you, move toward it instead of far from it (acknowledgment). We as a whole have torment in our lives, whether it's the ex despite everything we yearn for, the jackhammer growling over the road, or the sudden flood of uneasiness when we get up to give a discourse. On the off chance that we let them, such aggravations can divert us from the happiness regarding life. Incomprehensibly, the undeniable reaction—concentrating on the issue keeping in mind the end goal to battle and overcome it—frequently aggravates it.

12.To capitalize on time, forget about it (flow).Perhaps the most finish method for living at the time is the condition of aggregate ingestion therapists call stream. Stream happens when you're so immersed in an errand that you forget about everything else around you. Stream exemplifies an evident Catch 22: How would you be able to live at the time in case you not in any case mindful exist apart from everything else? The profundity of engagement assimilates you intensely, keeping consideration so engaged that diversions can't infiltrate. You concentrate so seriously on what you're doing that you're uninformed of the progression of time. Hours can go without you taking note.

13.Stream is a slippery state. Similarly as with sentiment or rest, you can't simply will yourself into it—everything you can do is set the stage, making the ideal conditions for it to happen.

14.To enhance your execution, quit contemplating it (unselfconsciousness).

I've never felt agreeable on a move floor. My developments feel cumbersome. I feel like individuals are passing judgment on me. I never recognize what to do with my arms. I need to give up, yet I can't, on the grounds that I know I look ludicrous. That is the primary mystery of living at the time: Thinking too hard about what you're doing really aggravates you do. In case you're in a circumstance that makes you restless—giving a discourse, acquainting yourself with a more interesting, moving—concentrating on your nervousness has a tendency to increase it.

15.Make cleaning and cooking your contemplation. Cooking and cleaning are regularly seen as drudgery, in any case they are both extraordinary approaches to practice care, and can be incredible customs performed every day. In the event that cooking and cleaning appear like exhausting errands to you, take a stab at doing them as a type of contemplation. Put your whole personality into those assignments, focus, and do them gradually and totally. It could change your whole day (and in addition go out). Continue rehearsing. When you get disappointed, simply take a full breath.

16.When you are conversing with somebody, be available, rationally and physically. What number of us have invested energy with somebody however have been supposing about what we have to do later on? Then again considering what we need to say next, rather than truly listening to that individual? Rather, concentrate on being available, on truly tuning in, on truly making the most of your time with that individual.

17.Spend no less than 5 minutes every day doing nothing. Simply sit peacefully. Gotten to be mindful of your considerations. Concentrate on your relaxing. Notice your general surroundings. Gotten to be OK with the quiet and stillness. It'll do you a ton of good - and just takes 5 minutes!

18.Put space between things. It's a method for dealing with your timetable so that you generally have room schedule-wise to finish every errand. Try not to timetable things near one another - rather, leave room between things on your calendar. That gives you a more casual calendar, and leaves space on the off chance that one errand takes longer than you arranged.

19. Eat gradually and enjoy your food. Food can be packed down our throats in a surge, however where's the delight in that? Enjoy every nibble, gradually, and truly get the most out of your sustenance. Strikingly, you'll eat less thusly, and condensation your sustenance better too.

20. Live gradually and flavor your life. Just as you would relish your nourishment by eating it all the more gradually, do all that along these lines - moderate down and appreciate every single minute. Tune into the sights and sounds and stir your faculties to your general surroundings.

If you practice these above tips on a daily basis, you are sure to notice a drastic improvement in your temperament. You will feel more alive and happy. You will also find yourself with renewed energy to do all the things you want to.

Chapter 8: Mindful Behavior

During the course of your days, you do things that take up your time and some things seem less important than others, although they are not. Every action that you take within the course of a day is equally important as it is eating a moment into your life. When you start to live life in a mindful way, you develop yourself. That's important because it means that you are more aware of your life and of all the wonderful things that surround you, even in times of difficulty. Let me explain to you how mindful behavior improves your life.

You may have something to do and instead of doing it, you choose to do something else. You may even multi task. The way that the brain works is that it's capable of doing one thing properly at a time. It doesn't much like multi-tasking and in fact, it tires you. If you take one little job and make yourself completely aware of what you are doing and absorb yourself in it, you are being mindful of what you are doing. For example, when you drink coffee, savor the aroma, feel the warmth of the cup, take a sip onto your tongue and let the coffee caress your taste buds. Don't just swallow and move on to doing something else. We tend to eat at a pace these days. Slow it down and enjoy every single taste and texture. You improve your health when you do that, but if you can apply the same mindfulness to each task that you undertake, you will feel better about having to do it and enjoy it more.

The element that makes your life now different from your life with mindfulness is judgment. You need to learn to put judgment out of the picture. If someone asks you to do something you don't really like doing, don't sweat the small stuff. Even things like cleaning floors can become wonder-worlds for the imagination and creativity. Be present in the moment and be with what you are doing completely, knowing that everything else is outside the scope of what you are doing. Enjoy watching the water on the floor and see how it glistens. Be aware of moving the cloth across the floor and the shine that it produces.

When you can see things happening in your life without judgment, you become more compassionate. For example, people may say things that would normally be intended to hurt you. If you judge that person and allow their words to hurt you, you gain nothing at all. If, however, you drop judgment and let the words flow over your head and become empathetic. Put yourself in the shoes of others. Their words don't have to affect you. Neither do you need to retort in anger. Simply accept what is, is. The benefit of this lack of judgment is that it allows you to let go when things are not exactly what you planned and also be able to see different people's viewpoints but place no real judgment on them, realizing that everyone has opinions and that they are entitled to them. Your opinions don't have to be swayed by them. You simply have to accept that there will always be differences between people and that those differences are there for a reason.

You need to learn to be compassionate with yourself. You learn to become a happier person when you work on the areas of your life that you feel need a little help. Are you attentive enough? Do you give as much as people give you? Do you approach life with a positive mindset? Write down the things you know are your weak points and think of one of these before you meditate and you will find that the subconscious mind is able to help you to find solutions. Your solutions don't lie in other people's approval of you, but in your own acceptance of yourself.

When you walk, be mindful of each step that your legs take. Look at the area you pass through and begin to notice things instead of having a head full of thoughts that make you miss all of the moments of your life that you should be enjoying. The two golden rules are these:

Your past has gone and there is nothing you can do to change it.

Your future has not yet arrived and may never come, so it's not worth sweating it.

Be in the moment. Be in the now.

"Looking at beauty in the world is the first step of purifying the mind." Amit Ray

In the next chapter, we touch on the spiritual side of mindfulness. Spirituality helps you to feel at one with nature. It makes you feel that you have a part to play in the world and helps you to step out of your shell to embrace life to its fullest. Even on the darkest winter day, there is joy to behold if you are mindful enough to grasp it with both hands and see what is in front of your eyes. Stop letting the world invade your mind with noise and take mindfulness with you on your journey through life because it helps you to feel more complete.

Chapter 9: Practice Mindful Breathing

Your breath is the essence of your life. One of the physiological changes triggered by the stress response is the shift of normal breathing to rapid, shallow breathing, which in turn sets off anxiety. When stress and anxiety become a constant in your life, you slowly build the habit of taking shallow, rapid breaths. This in turn signals your mind to set off the stress response at all times so unknowingly, you stay in a constant state of stress and anxiety.

To let go of the undue stress and anxiety circulating in your body and mind, it is paramount to correct your breathing first. By practicing mindful breathing, you learn to become more aware of your breath and slowly convert it to deep, relaxed breathing from shallow, rapid breathing. This according to science produces many healthy results in your body such as improved sleep, stronger heart and a drop in blood pressure.

Further, when you learn to breathe mindfully, you start living more in the present moment instead of lurking in the past or future. When you stop thinking about how painful the past was or what the future may have in store for you, you only enjoy the present and make the best use of it.

Here is how you can practice mindfulness based breathing and slowly train yourself to breathe the right way.

How to Breathe Mindfully

·Begin by sitting or lying down comfortably on your exercise mat, couch or directly on the floor. You can sit or lie down in any pose that is comfortable for you. Make yourself comfortable when you sit or lie down.

· Close your eyes and then very slowly and gently, bring your attention to your breath.

· Your job now is to just observe your breath and bring every ounce of your awareness to it to feel and observe nothing but your breath.

· Breathe just as you normally do and there is no need to deepen or lengthen your breath. Your breath will naturally become deep with time if you consistently practice this exercise.

· Inhale through your nose and exhale through your mouth, and focus on how your breath enters your body, how it moves around in it and how it leaves your system.

· As you inhale and exhale, analyze where you feel it the most in your body and how it makes you feel.

· Your awareness may wander away every now and then since you don't have the habit of being aware of your breath and aren't mindful yet. This is perfectly normal and when this happens, don't be harsh with yourself. Mindfulness is about gently accepting everything and being at peace with it so when you find yourself wandering off in thought, just acknowledge that thinking just occurred and your awareness moved to something else, and then just gently bring back your attention to your breath. You can also count your breath to stay more focused on it. Do it a few times and you won't have much trouble focusing on your breath again.

Do this exercise for about 10 minutes. Over time, increase the duration of the practice. When you end the practice, do it very gently and slowly bring back your attention to everything around you. You will feel a lot calmer and peaceful than before. You will also feel less stressed than before. This is the magic of being mindful and breathing mindfully.

Practice mindfulness based breathing every morning when you wake up and before starting your routine work. This ensures you start your day with clarity, increased focus and peacefulness. Carry it out once more before going to bed to sleep peacefully. For about 2 weeks, practice mindfulness based breathing when you start and end your day. Once you feel more adjusted to it, do it more often in the day too especially when you feel stressed or before doing an important chore. The more you do it, the better you will get at it. Also, this reinforces your habit of breathing the right way. Soon, you will always be breathing mindfully and will be better aware of everything around you.

To become fully mindful, it is important to observe and listen to things mindfully because only when you start observing and listening to things nonjudgmentally, you will become more accepting of different things. The next chapter tells you exactly how you can do that.

Chapter 10: Where To Practice Mindfulness?

We could laughingly say, much like the last chapter, that "mindfulness can be done anywhere!" Well, that is true, but let me explain. Mindfulness is something that we can do while sitting in the doctor's office, standing in line at the grocery store, or even just walking to the bathroom. But it also something which we can devote time to. One can dedicate a specific place where they find they are the most mindful and can also meet with certain people that help them feel grounded or mindful. This is natural, as for thousands of years humans have associated certain places and people with spirituality or mindfulness. It is common for people to go to church for religious worship and we can even go back in history to certain parts of a forest used as monuments for rituals. We've always assembled in places which provide us with the spiritual and emotional energy we need to carry on in the world. While some of these are still present, people often find themselves reaching an epiphany in less significant locations as well. For example, you may have a person who finds herself most happy running on the treadmill or you may have a person who is most at peace taking a drive in the hills. Some people go to church, while others meditate on a rock in their backyard. All of these examples act as location for the person to be able to experience some spiritual energy. Doing things such as this bring us to a different state of mind. It is like a racecar driver goes into a different state of mind when they put on their helmet. They are supposed to be calm, alert, aware and hyper-focused to be able to notice things at 200 miles per hour. Where to practice mindfulness will be up the individual person in the sense that some people will prefer quiet, no noise, or no bothers while another person will most appreciate the birds and animal sounds of nature. Some may even prefer sounds of the street, with cars and people walking about. None of these examples are wrong and where they find peace is entirely up to them. Before deciding where to practice a mindful exercise, you will need to ask yourself some important questions. First of all, are you the kind of person who can hear your own inner voice telling you how you're doing despite your surroundings or are you someone who needs silence and focus to hear your inner self? Secondly, where (physically, in your world) are you most able to focus on something? Are you the kind of person to study in a quiet library corner or the kind of person who sits down the most popular coffee shop in town to read a book? Where you like to return to study something or read something is a good indicator about where the best place for you to practice might be.

Let's get a little more in-depth to help better define the kind of place you'll need. As a basic recommendation, find a quiet place to sit in a comfortable chair. Try to sit with your back straight and your feet flat on the floor, with thighs parallel to the floor and hands in your lap. Keep your head straight up, as if being pulled up by a string. As you sit, make sure you are in a position to be able to take deep breaths. You can also try sitting in the classic legs-crossed position. To do so, following the above but sit on the floor and cross your legs however is comfortable, either with your feet under each other, with one on top of a knee, or fully crossed with your feet placed on top of each other knee. Consider using a large pillow or cushion to sit on. Other things to consider about where you practice mindfulness include access to your other senses. For example, having something nearby that smells good (like incense or a scented candle) or having something that feels good like a fluffy blanket to wrap around yourself, can be comforting and help access the present moment. The most important thing to remember is that where you do mindfulness is not necessarily as important as how it is done. Where you do it could be considered the preparation point that helps you get into a mindful place quickly and effectively. Now that you can be prepared, you can move into the specific mindful exercises.

Chapter 11: Control Shyness And Social Anxiety

In this chapter, we intend to examine how to get over shyness. Shyness results in numerous uncomfortable side effects in persons living. It could alter their association with other individuals. It can affect their self-worth. It can stop someone's personal development. There are plenty of techniques for getting over shyness. Below are a few tips to make it easier to when you're combating shyness.

There are numerous stellar self-help programs available that can assist you to get a superior knowledge with regards to your shyness. These types of self-help programs can provide some insight on how to cope and defeat shyness. By simply checking out self-help programs you'll have a greater probability of succeeding. These programs can provide you with directions about how as well as what to do to prevail over shyness.

Hunt down folks that could support you on the journey. Having a support group can keep you pushed and motivated to get to your desired goals. Uncover friends and family that you can rely on. Find those that will certainly propel you to ultimately be successful. Tend not to surround yourself with those who put you down. Surround yourself with people who will certainly promote you to become your better self. Make sure you pick these folks wisely. Ensure that the people you decide on are constructive. Set yourself up to succeed.

If you do not feel comfortable looking for help, well then hunt down guidance from specialists. Specialists assistance can be extremely beneficial in assisting you to control shyness. You'll find several masters in the particular field. After a little study, it is possible to discover a skilled professional who will help you. Maybe you might even make an effort to look for help in your local area. If this isn't possible then make an online search as an instrument to find a professional that you're comfortable with.

These are merely a few strategies on how to get over shyness. Shyness is not just intending to disappear altogether on its own. It takes a little effort, but it's well worth it. Attempt to see whether there is a self-help program that you find comforting. Coming across people today to give you support may help make certain your ability to succeed. You may ask for specialist help if you feel more comfortable going that way. The option depends on what you decide. To beat shyness, you will need to opt for what you feel safe trying and you've got to be able to take that 1st step.

We're all shy at times. Often when there's a new situation that we're not sure of. Or when there's some pressure on us like going on a date with someone for the first time. Here are some easy ways to control your shyness.

Pay attention to the other person

Usually, our shyness is because we think the other person won't like us. Pay attention to them (not in a creepy way!). Listen to what they're saying rather than constantly thinking about what you're going to say next - there's plenty of time to do that once you've listened to the other person.

Do this a few times and tailor your conversation to what the other person has said - rather than what you thought they might have said - and you'll be well on your way to controlling your shyness because you'll be on the receiving end of nice people who want to interact with you.

Learn to relax and stop tensing up

Quite often tension goes hand in hand with shyness.

We come over "all shy" and then we tense up when we realize what we're doing.

That brings out the killer instinct in a lot of other people. They sense weakness and prey on it.

Take some time out to practice relaxation techniques in private and then use an "anchor" such as squeezing your thumb and middle finger together to allow you to reach something close to that relaxed state at literally your fingertips.

While you're learning to do this, the short term just takes some nice, long, deep breaths as this will help to calm you down.

When you're a bit calmer, you'll bring down your shyness level almost automatically.

Stop trying to be so perfect

Perfectionism is a disease. And it brings on lots of side effects, one of which is nervousness and shyness because you want to cover up your lack of perfectionism.

When you chill out and realize that you're human (or at least, I'm assuming you are for this section!) you can relax into the situation, let your shyness dissolve and show your true colors.

Visualize stuff

Day dream a bit - it's allowed.

See your shyness melting away or floating off on the breeze. If it's not too embarrassing, physically wave goodbye to it. Otherwise just pretend that's what you're doing.

Let your mind run riot. Maybe see your shyness being chased off by the Wily Coyote and delight in the way that it fights back with the traditional Acme dynamite.

Have a wild time with this. If the people around you start asking why you're laughing out loud, you're somewhere close to the right spot. And answering their questions will help chase your shyness even further away.

Torture yourself in public

Not literally of course.

Just metaphorically.

Choose a non-threatening situation to do this - somewhere you're not usually visiting, that kind of thing.

Then be the most outward going person you can be, even if it's just for a minute or two.

This will "rub off" into normal situations and you'll find your defensive shield of shyness starting to drop away and the real you starting to shine through.

Sited in a classroom among your own classmates can evoke apprehension, especially if it involves standing up to address them. This scenario is not just limited to the classroom; it could involve any situation where much people are involved. The heartbeat gets faster, the palms and limbs feel sweaty and shaky etc, these are signs of social anxiety. Social anxiety is a common phenomenon among young people today. It is a limiting and inferiority complex that can negatively affect productivity and output of a person. In some instances, an individual is likely to experience anxiety includes: meeting new people, standing and speaking before a group of people, engaging in an activity that includes people watching you e.g.

participating in a sporting activity, excursions, class discussions etc. The awkward issue about social anxiety is that most of its sufferers are often aware of the issue but are helpless in overcoming it.

How to overcome social anxiety

1. Work on your mind: Social anxiety is a complex that is rooted in perception and feeling of inferiority to others around. Therefore, the solution to social anxiety must start from the mind. The individual must recognize that all people are the same and no one is special or better than the other. This is important because without it overcoming social anxiety will continue to be a mirage.

2. Get involved: Problem identified is already half way solved, so says the popular proverb. Since social anxiety involves being anxious about social settings and situations, it follows that in order to overcome it, engaging in the social activity is key. It is important that if an individual must overcome anxiety, they should further get involved in the social

activity. The individual should immerse themselves more into social settings, with time; they will eventually overcome the menace.

3. Hypnosis: Hypnosis is an induced sense of relaxation that helps an individual focus and concentrate better. It is useful in treating a variety of psychological issues prominent among which is social anxiety. One option for hypnosis is to see a professional. Many people these days, especially with a difficult problem like social anxiety, feel they would like to take a crack at healing themselves.

Remember how it was mentioned to find who you want to be? That still applies and is a major part of the self-hypnosis process to overcome your phobia.

Here are a few helpful tips to get going (how to overcome social anxiety):

•Write down positive things about yourself

• Start small and push away any negative thoughts

- Next, take note of a handful of situations that could improve without social anxiety.
- Remind yourself of these qualities and goals constantly.

Following these steps, you can begin the hypnosis process. These are the basics for how to overcome social anxiety with self-hypnosis:

- Find a quiet, peaceful place where you can go for at least 30 minutes.
- While sitting comfortably, close your eyes and breathe deeply, focusing on relaxing.
- Count down slowly from ten, imagining something like an elevator or cracks in a sidewalk.
- At count one, a door opens. Imagine whatever you need there and include your list.
- Continue to breathe deeply and say anything aloud if you think it helps.
- When you are ready, leave the room and count slowly upward to ten.

- At count ten, slowly open your eyes and feel the power in your suggestions and calm.

Next time you wonder if you'll ever feel comfortable socially, hypnosis may help you. It is even a solution for how to overcome the social anxiety that you can do on your own.

Chapter 12: Preparing For Mindfulness

The problem with trying to jump into mindfulness is that it's not possible or plausible. You need to learn all about silence in your mind and learn relaxation. People who are stressed don't usually know how to relax. If you want to make the most of meditation, you need to be able to do these things. This is why I thought that this chapter would help you. Close your eyes and try to think of absolutely nothing. See how long you can last. It's quite possible that you may last a couple of minutes, but it's more likely to be seconds because you are not accustomed to thinking of nothing.

Now try something else. Lie down on a bed with your head supported and making sure that your clothing is comfortable. This should be in a room where there is no distraction. For example, if the TV is going in the next room, turn it off. You need silence so that you can concentrate on this exercise that will help you toward learning mindful meditation.

Close your eyes and breathe in through the nose, hold the breath for a moment and breathe out. On the breathing outward, you should feel the breath coming from your upper abdomen but people get very lazy about the way that they breathe. To ensure that the air is coming from the right place, place a hand on your diaphragm and feel it pivot as you breathe.

When you are accustomed to this style of breathing, concentrate totally on your toes. Tense them and feel conscious of them being tensed and then relax them. Continue to concentrate on your toes as they begin to feel heavier and more relaxed. Work your way through all the parts of your body, thinking of nothing else at all. Your toes are followed by your ankles, your calf, your knee, your thigh, your hips, your waist, your chest, your neck, your hands, your wrists, your elbows, your shoulders and then your head.

As you think of each part of the body, tense it and then relax it, going through the same process for every part of your body until you feel totally at ease and relaxed.

The reason why this exercise is important to meditation is because it makes you think of nothing outside of the thought of the part of the body that you are trying to relax. Thus, you are already thinking in that moment. When your foot tensed, you felt it. When it relaxed, you felt it. You put your heart and soul into the relaxation process and thought of nothing else at all. This is great practice for preparing for mindful meditation because it's difficult to let go of thoughts.

In the early stages of doing this exercise, you can be forgiven if your mind wanders, though practice it again and again, for about 20 minutes a day and if you find yourself thinking about anything at all that isn't in that very moment, go back to your toes and start again.

This exercise is also beneficial from a relaxation and sleep point of view. If you are stressed, perhaps you are not sleeping as well as you should be. You may not know it but during sleep the body releases all kinds of hormones that heal the body and mind and if you are depriving yourself of sleep, you deprive yourself of this valuable healing as well. This, while you are preparing to start meditation, it's a good idea to try and get sufficient sleep at night. You need about eight hours. Sometimes, thought processes get in the way of sleep and especially if you are stressed. You do need to switch off at night and perhaps the following exercise will help you.

Sleep exercise

For this exercise, close your eyes and imagine yourself behind the steering wheel of your car. Imagine all the actions that you take such as:

- Look in mirror
- Put key in ignition
- Turn key
- Put car in gear
- Look around
- Move off

Try to think of a route that you know by heart. See all the familiar sights and keep driving making yourself go through all the motions that you would do such as stopping at a T junction, etc. Because this is something that people do without even thinking about it, it's a great exercise for getting off to sleep. Chances are that you won't even reach your destination. If you find yourself thinking about other things, discipline yourself and go back to the beginning again.

Remember that late night TV may upset your sleep patterns if it is too active and that you may not be sleeping because you ate too late. Try to avoid this so that you do get enough relaxation, as this really will help your stress levels to lower.

Repeat the exercises shown in this chapter a few times and really get into the swing of turning off your thoughts, as this helps you to prepare for meditation. When you finish a relaxation session, don't get up too quickly. Let your body slowly come back to its normal state by opening your eyes and rising very slowly from your relaxation exercise.

You need to get used to doing that because it's very much the same when you start to meditate. You never push yourself back into chaos straight after a meditation session. Taking it slowly helps you to gain the most benefit that you can from your meditation.

Chapter 13: The Mindfulness Experience

In order to avoid the monotony of having to practice the same kind of meditation every time, it is ideal to consider a more diverse program, which includes various kinds of exercises designed to increase mindfulness. For instance, if you wonder how you could color one week of your life, so that you can have the opportunity to enjoy your mindfulness experience each day, you could organize your program into different kinds of exercises. Thus, you train your mind to yield to the present moment through other means each day. Please keep in mind it is important not to be neglectful with your practices. Meditating once in a while is good enough, but perhaps you should start with a more complex application of the concept of mindfulness in your life. For this purpose you can try out the following plan.

Day 1

You can start with the body scan, an exercise that helps you pay minute attention to every part of your body. Start from the top of your head and let your thought descend on every part of your body in a systematic and careful way as you try to be as perceptive as possible to any kind of sensation you may experience in that particular area. For instance, what does your hair feel like? If it's medium length and it falls on your neck, what does it feel like when it touches your skin? What is the shape of your shoulders? Can you feel it with your own thought focus as you gently scan them mentally? What does the tissue of your clothes feel like? Do you have any sensation in your nails? Can you feel the back of your thighs with the opposite leg as you sit in your classic meditation position? Try going as slowly as you can over each body part, settling your thoughts on your palpable flesh and what your senses tell you. Do this for over 15 minutes – linger as if you caressed each part of your body with your mind.

Day 2

A second mindfulness experience is 'the raisin exercise'. You should start with mere observation. Take a raisin in your hand and notice anything you can about it: texture, color, shape etc. Touch it and let your palm feel the sensations. Then after you have felt it with your skin, let it burst on your tongue. Explore its taste slowly, trying to immerse in what your taste buds tell you. This is a simple exercise that brings you back in the present moment by stimulating several of your senses and making you use them in a very aware way. Of course you can try it with different kinds of food, but ideally you should use something you don't eat every day, which can be appealing to your senses in several ways: e.g. figs, avocado, papaya, kiwi, cashews, almond, pistachio, etc. It's optimal to limit yourself to one type of food during an exercise, so as to fully revel in its unique taste. If you use something like pistachio, for instance, you can let your senses and your mind linger on all its aspects: both the shell and the seed. Of course you can start with a something simple such as a fig or a cashew seed, but it also works if you go on with slices of kiwi or papaya. You can start by feeling the whole fruit with its soft skin; then slowly peel it noticing its smell and its texture with the tips of your fingers. Eventually let the flesh melt on your tongue and enjoy the taste to the fullest.

Day 3

The Walking exercise can be done inside a large room or a corridor. However, it may actually be more effective if you practice it outside. Make sure you are in a very tranquil and quiet area such as a park, a garden, a forest walk, the bank of a lake, etc. You shouldn't be disturbed by noise in any way. The key to this exercise is following each of your steps as you take it – lose yourself in the rhythm of your own steps. Focus on the movement of your body as if in slow motion. Pay attention to any slight contraction of your muscles as you raise your leg, then place it back on the ground. You can also count your steps slowly. You should start by pacing along a path where you can take 20-30 steps, then return to the initial place. Repeat for as long as you feel comfortable. However, don't do it automatically, try to consciously follow the slight tension of your steps as you let your legs move and touch the ground. By becoming aware of such a common activity that we usually take for granted, you will enhance your mindfulness experience.

Day 4

On the 4th day of your mindfulness program for beginners, you can practice a quite simple, but immensely pleasurable exercise. Dedicate 5-10 minutes of your life to observing the nature you can see from one of your windows. Are you taking a break from work? Have you just arrived back home from school? Are you just cooking something and as you wait for the food to be ready, you wonder what you should do to avoid boredom? Many of us are accustomed to 'fill in' such time by checking our FB pages or our e-mail inbox. How many of us actually listen to a relaxing and beautiful piece of music in such moments? That would be great to do. However, for your purpose of increasing mindfulness, here's something even more beneficial. Take your time to look outside your window and let your gaze follow and perceive all the details of whatever you can spot in your environment: let your eyes follow the contours of clouds or trees; watch leaves as they fall to the ground, if it's autumn; try to absorb flowers and trees in bloom slowly during spring; follow a butterfly or a bird in the sky and pay attention to any movement such a creature makes etc. Allow yourself such breaks as often as you can. It will bring you 'down to earth' into the present moment in the most concrete way possible. You will realize how many things you actually let pass by due to ignorance or stress.

Day 5

The next exercise implies a simple 'game' in which you let fresh air 'vibrate' on your exposed skin. You can take 5-10 minutes and go outside or stay at your window while you follow the touch of air on your skin. For instance, you can expose your arms or your feet. Let your body feel the air, as you probably never do, because it seems something so banal. If the wind is blowing, take advantage of extra air movement and let it 'play' on your skin as you try to feel each sensation.

Day 6

This exercise is an interesting variation of the previous one. You will use water instead of air this time. Of course you can do it in the shower while letting water freely move on your skin. However, it is recommended and more pleasant to try it when you are outside, in the middle of nature, near a lake, a spring, or some other kind of water source (e.g. a fountain in a park). But, since such places may not be as easily accessible, the you can generate a worthy experience while outside using a hose, which can give you the added sensation of the air outside versus a shower indoors. Let your skin enjoy the feel of water for at least 5 minutes. Of course you should make sure the water is not too cold …although a little cold would actually improve the quality of the sensation and increase your focus on what you can feel. Ideally, you should have access to some kind of water that is a bit colder than your skin. You can move your hand or your arm slowly as the water touches your skin, as if enjoying the sensation from several angles. Needless to say, what a wonderful experience you can have if you do such a thing when it rains. However, we cannot control or predict weather so well to afford including it in our mindfulness plan. What you can do is never hesitate to take advantage of the moment whenever it rains in a pleasant and moderate way (especially during spring or summer). Take 5-10 minutes of your time and turn them into a wonderful mindfulness experience!

Day 7

The Loving-kindness meditation starts from an amazingly efficient idea developed by Sylvia Boorstein. It is an exercise of self-love and other-love that shows you how connected these two forms are. Start by articulating what you desire most for yourself in your mind: e.g. may I be happy; may I have a life full of love; may I be successful and strong, etc. Direct these affirmations with the power of thought towards yourself, first of all. The next step is to think of someone you like and wish them the same things, directing the beneficial positive energy in the form of clear thoughts and wishes towards them. Expand this to someone you may have considered yourself to be indifferent to. Proceed with people you may actually think you dislike. By spreading your positive emotional energy and thoughts around people instead of being judgmental, you actually engage in a profound mindfulness experience. In the end, direct the same wishes through powerfully felt thoughts to everyone around you – all people in the world, humanity at large, or any other kind of being you may come across (as long as it means 'spirit' to you). This extremely fulfilling and complex exercise should be wholeheartedly felt to be potent. Not only does it teach you how to focus your thoughts on concrete people and feelings you choose, but also it boosts your energy and dispels any negativity you may have experienced. Thus, it helps you transform your own emotional energy and thought patterns and it fills you with joy and appreciation of what you have instead of intolerance, indifference, or dislike. For more details on this meditation idea, check out the following video:

Chapter 14: Mindfulness In Managing Your Life

When you lose your temper, the person who suffers the most is you. Learn to observe your life and when you feel any kind of negativity coming into your mind, try to distance yourself from it. You can use the "Letting go" system or you can give yourself something more concrete to occupy your mind. Personally, I think that people new to mindfulness will be more adept at replacement tactics. For example, someone says something that you would normally react to during the course of your working day. This is something negative. Do not respond. Simply acknowledge what was said and then look around you and observe things that are happening in this moment.

Perhaps you have access to a window where you can look out and see things happening. You need to awaken all of your senses. Your sense of taste, smell, touch, hearing, sight should all be used to the betterment of your life. Instead of thinking about the negative thing that someone said and dissecting it until it makes no more sense, drop it straight away. You are wasting your energy if you are letting negative behavior on the part of someone else become your problem.

Take ownership of the moments in your life. Use them in such a way that you enjoy them and savor them. For example, if you are accustomed to eating on the go, stop to eat your sandwiches and taste every bite, feeling the different textures and tastes and make sure that you chew your food sufficiently. This will help your digestive system to feel better. Use your senses to see the flowers in the park and enjoy them instead of having so much in your life and in your mind that you don't have time to enjoy this very moment.

The things that you don't have time for in your life are the following:

Negative moments of thought

Negative memories

Negative people

However, for the last item on that list, try to be more empathetic and understand that what people say and how they are feeling is something that you maybe don't have a full understanding of. Let their words enter your mind, if you need to act on them, do so, but if you don't need to take any action, simply let go. You fuel your own negativity and anxiety as well as adding to your stress levels when you hold on to negativity and keep on thinking in negative terms. Remember, mindfulness is all about being non-judgmental.

Look around you as an exercise in mindfulness. Take note of your surroundings and then close your eyes for a few moments. Can you describe what you saw? Try it because you may find that you missed a lot of detail. The reason for this is because although we are present in our lives, often our minds are elsewhere. I would suggest that a way of reinforcing the importance of living in the moment would be to set your alarm clock half an hour earlier, sit down and enjoy your breakfast, but before doing this, go out into the garden. Look to see if there are any dew drops in the garden that have clung to cobwebs because these are a beauty to behold that you may not have seen before. Perhaps the dewdrops are still there on rose petals. If you don't have a garden, what about the park on the way to work? Make sure you get to see the world around you because it's there for you to enjoy. If your thoughts are of other times and other places, you are not actually making the most of that moment in time.

I would suggest that you also read some inspirational works. One particular book that I have in mind is by the philosopher Khalil Gibran and it's a book called The Prophet. It's not about religion. It is about attitudes to life and if you can surround yourself with inspiration in your life, you will find that gradually, stress and anxiety disappear into the background and you begin to find life enjoyable and rewarding.

Chapter 15: The Top Ten Tips For Being Mindful

Now that we have seen the top 10 best possible ways to indulge in mindfulness meditation, let us take a look at the top 10 tips that will help us be all the more mindful, so that we can take that mindfulness experience of ours to an altogether unprecedented level.

The top 10 tips for being Mindful

#1 Understand that thoughts are nothing but thoughts.

A lot of times we make the mistake of assuming that our thoughts exert a great deal of control over us. The only reason that they ever do exert any control, is because we allow them to. We need to understand that they are simply thoughts and that we don't have to believe them or react to them in any which way.

#2 Don't ever give up.

You will find that it takes some time to cultivate the level of mindfulness that you will like to have, and if in the beginning your mind is flooded with thoughts and emotions you need not worry. As you persist and keep getting better in your practice, those thoughts will become lesser and lesser.

#3 Don't go too hard on yourself as far as that meditation is concerned.

You might think that if you are to be meditating, you need to do it for at least one hour a day. This might cause you to refrain from trying out some of the fun meditations we have discussed in the earlier chapter, like the shower and eating meditations. The very fact that these meditations have made it to the list is because you really don't need to set aside all that much time for your meditation. Try doing it for five minutes at first, and then extend it to fifteen minutes. You really don't need more than fifteen minutes a day for a great mindfulness meditation.

#4 Engage your senses more and more with the things around you.

You will see that mindfulness is not merely restricted to your meditative practice; rather, it is a way of life. You need to ensure that you engage completely with things around you, be it smelling a flower or listening to the sound of the rain outside.

#5 Practice it in the morning for the best results.

When you practice mindfulness first thing in the morning, you will see that it sets the tone for the day to come, thus making it all the more probable to be mindful in the later hours of the day. It doesn't have to be a sitting meditation right after you wake up; it could even be that commute meditation we have talked about. Don't wait until night to indulge in that mindfulness meditation of yours.

#6 Stop fiddling with your smartphone every now and then.

One of the biggest reasons why people find themselves unable to actually be in the present is because they are taking away the very beauty of the moment they find themselves in, through the act of incessantly being engaged with their smartphones. Set aside a time everyday that you can assign to checking

your social media, and while you might wish to answer calls, don't turn to that smartphone every now and then merely to check how many likes you might have gotten for that last picture you posted. Be in the moment and appreciate it instead – like perhaps when you are walking down the street and observing the beautiful sights and sounds around you.

#7 Simply watch people.

You don't have to only be on your way to work in order to watch people as part of your mindfulness practice, as we have already discussed. In fact, you could watch people wherever you are, be it in a café or perhaps even at the stadium when you are watching a game. Observe them and imagine what they might be doing in their lives or the kind of people they might be. That's a great way to be mindful and a lot of fun too!

#8 Practice it while you are waiting.

A lot of times you find yourself waiting for inordinately long periods of time, such as when you are at the doctor's office or perhaps even in the line at your local Starbucks. You need to make sure that you utilize the extra time on your

hands by being more mindful, simply by observing all the things around you (this is another great chance to observe people as well). That will certainly make your wait more than worthwhile!

#9 Don't multitask.

You might think that this is an impossible thing to do, especially in a world that's as frenetically paced as ours. However, the truth is that when you multitask you are really not doing justice to the tasks you are performing and neither are you getting much joy in the process. So, while you are sitting at that breakfast table you might not wish to reach for that spoonful of cereal that you won't even see entering your mouth. Instead, read the paper after you have finished eating breakfast (preferably in the mindful manner we have touched upon).

#10 Increase concentration in those areas you find yourself drifting away.

There are times when you will find yourself drifting away in your mind when you are performing a certain activity, like perhaps taking your dog for a walk or checking your email. These are the very times that you should increase your degree of focus, so that you are mindful while you are doing them. This

will only serve to make you all the more mindful and ensure that very soon you will have reached a stage where you don't have to prompt yourself every now and then to be mindful.

Chapter 16: Mindfulness In Everyday Life

We already know what mindfulness is but how can you put it into practice in your everyday life? Well, it's simple. Be present in everything that you do. For example, if you make it a routine to get up in the morning and meditate for 20 minutes, you can then start your day with your mind clear as a bell and able to absorb all the things that are happening within your life. When you go to take your breakfast, make enough time to sit down and enjoy it. Smell the aroma of the coffee. Let it sit on your tongue and enjoy it. When you eat your breakfast, take time to eat. Don't rush through this moment as if you haven't got time to enjoy your food. Chew it properly. Let your mouth feel all of the textures and tastes of your food. Your stomach will be calmer for it and you may find yourself enjoying eating for the first time in a long time.

Be with your family first thing in the morning and be present with them. That means instead of mumbling to each other over the newspaper, you take an active interest in their days, what they are wearing and how they are feeling. We rush through life and forget that all of these small moments matter. If you want to eliminate worry from your life, you have to simply tell yourself each time that you worry that this worry does not pertain to this moment, so is irrelevant. Replace worry with presence. Let me explain that. If you are scrubbing the kitchen floor and find yourself worried about something that is happening tomorrow, step back into mindfulness. Watch every move of the scrubbing brush. Feel the floor getting cleaner, concentrate on the moment. Not only will you make a better job of the floor, but you will be able to put worry aside. When you are worrying while walking through the park, step into the moment and look at the plants. A worry is only there while you allow it to be. Thus, replace it with all the scents and feelings that you get from this place. All of your senses should be experienced to the full.

In this moment, see the flowers, touch a petal, smell the perfume, taste the freshness of the air. By making yourself aware of everything that is happening in this moment, you take away the possibility of worrying.

You need to recognize in your own life the triggers for worry and make sure that you replace them. Thus, you should go through your life being very aware of everything around you. Look at the color of the leaves on the trees. Go somewhere you find spectacular and simply sit there and be still. What you will find is that this is a wonderful reminder of the subtlety of change. You will also be reminded about how small you are and that's never a bad thing. When you see yourself as a smaller part of the universe, you actually get to appreciate how each small part of the universe comes together to make a whole universe and it doesn't matter how small you are. You are just as important as the larger parts of the universe. Imagine yourself as a grain of sand and learn that humility is a wonderful thing. Just because you see yourself as tiny as that grain of sand, you must know that without all those individual grains of sand, there would be no beach.

Mindfulness means tasting life as it happens and that's so important. Be kind to yourself and be kind to those around you. This moment is the most important and significant moment of your life, whatever you are doing, because it's all that you have to hold onto. Once it has passed, you can never relive it and there's not much point in having regrets because that takes you out of the moment and back into thinking about time that has already gone. Sit in the open air. Breathe the air and allow your body and soul to enjoy the moment for everything that it is. Perhaps you have people coming to dinner who irritate you. Be in the moment and you will see that all the pettiness of life takes a back seat. You can laugh at life and find your own happiness in that moment. Listen to music and allow your sense of hearing to feel the joy of every note. Mindfulness includes using your senses to better grasp this moment and if you need to relax, lie down and relax and use the breathing methods I have told you about to help you to be completely in that moment.

The amount of stress that people suffer in this day and age is frightening. Don't allow yourself to become victim of it. The Buddhist philosophy goes much deeper than this but once you grasp mindfulness, you appreciate even the most difficult of company because it helps you to understand that the world is made up of all kinds of people and that sometimes people we consider to be an irritation actually remind us to be better people than we show ourselves to be. If there were no bad people, there would be nothing to measure ourselves against. Thus, be compassionate and try to show those people who are in your life a way forward that is better for them without dictating anything. You never know, those people may be just as stressed as you have been in the past and your kindness could help them into the next moment of calm.

Mindfulness means being aware of every movement of your body, every step that you take, every breath that comes from within your lungs. Feel the air that you breathe and know that if you center your consciousness in the present, knowing that everything is transient, you are less likely to get caught up in stress and depression. In fact, you will be enthused by your own life and this will be reflected in the company you keep and the way you deal with your life in such a positive way. It is infectious and you can spread happiness and joy instead of always being the one who has bad news, or has something negative to share with people. If you find the time, it's worthwhile watching some of the YouTube videos made by the Dalai Lama as he is great at teaching people all about being present in their lives and using mindfulness as a way to be happier.

Chapter 17: Mindfulness For Physical Troubles

In the language of vipassanāvāda, the soul and the body are not two separate entities. Modern medicine tends to separate these two. The afflictions of the body are to be treated separately than the problems of the mind. Why is it so when both of these are equally important? We are not trying to undermine modern medicine. It has achieved great feats and has made life easier and simpler for so many people around the globe. Look at diabetes for example, the production of insulin via genetic engineering is no less than a miracle for people whose pancreas have failed them. So if you are a doctor and are reading this, do not be offended. We are not trying to challenge your art. Instead we claim that a mindful mind can work alongside the wondrous medicines that science has created for a more well-rounded and complete treatment.

Anyone who suffers from chronic pain can relate to the fact that pain drastically limits the options in your life. You have to plan your activities according to the nature and severity of the pain that you suffer from. Migraine is perhaps the most notorious of all the chronic pains. It can take over your life like a parasite and make you feel suffocated and restricted. Medicines are a temporary relief as there is no treatment available. On top of that there is the constant uncertainty as to when the crushing wave of pain might hit you.

So can mindfulness relieve or lessen the excruciating pain? Not Really.

What it can do is to help you regain control of your life that chronic pain has taken away from you. It can free you of that feeling of helplessness that you can no longer do what your heart feels like.

One of the many things that worries patients suffering from any chronic illness is the ultimate question of what will happen if they die? What will happen if their bodily functions are impaired? Another thing that can drown them in misery is the memory of the days when they were well and happy. They can drown in the ocean's lost dreams that were not realized because they were postponed to another time. They remember the places they did not visit, the things they did not get to say, the experience they did not get to have and resultantly a horrific guilt takes over them. A guilt born from lost opportunities and unrealized potential.

Guilt has no place within a mindful individual. Guilt is a notion of the past. It is a feeling associated things that have long gone.

Mindfulness preaches to live in the moment of now, no matter how painful that moment is. What makes illness all the more trying an experience is the constant comparison that is going on in the patient's mind between his/her state during illness and the one before he/she was stuck by the impairment.

This constant comparison gives a sense of loss that further develops into depression. Practicing mindfulness and being constantly aware of your body and the body of the universe will prevent the physical symptoms developing into a mental ailment.

Another important technique performed in mindfulness is the practice of active concentration. Actively concentrating on any one specific aspect, even if it is a word of God or prayer will divert the attention of the patient from the ongoing agony of pain. Concentrating on things that are well instead of pain can lessen the force felt by many measures. Connecting actively with the body of the universe will make the patient appreciate the beauty offered by the nature.

The sunshine still warms your face, you can feel the wind blowing against your cheek, you can smell freshly mown grass and you can still smile at all these things. Instead of wallowing over the loss of what you once had. Be content with all the countless blessings that you can still experience.

Religious men (and women) advise the followers to "count their blessings", which is actually the same as actively concentrating on what you have instead of what you have lost.

Remember how we earlier talked about the human need of constant competition? Being sick and unwell does not cure humans from this dark need. Instead it takes a more menacing form. The comparison between your own sick life and the seemingly happy life of others can drown you in depression as opposed to naked ambition. There is no room for this kind of competition for an individual who is actively mindful of his state. A mindful individual will realize that all humans, no matter how well or sick are a part of the body of the universe. Since it is all interconnected, the positivity of health can be absorbed into your body as well since it is after all coming from the same source. With active mindfulness, the vitality of others can actually be used to improve your condition as opposed to treating it as a source of resentment.

When you think of a phrase such as "fighting the disease", the first disease in question that comes to mind is the deadly Cancer. We all have heard that to truly defeat cancer willpower is just as important as the treatment you're under going. If you or anyone near you (Lord forbid) is fighting this many headed monster, then mindfulness can provide you with that surge of will and dedication to get this menace out of your system.

Taking small baby steps towards a more mindful existence is equivalent to taking small steps towards a healthier life.

Chapter 18: The Power Of Breathing

Breathing is something we all do all the time and because of that, we often don't even realize we are doing it but when we breathe we fill our cells with energy. Not only that, our breath is a root for us, it connects us to the earth, to nature, and to the Universe.

How can being aware of the breath help us?

We can use our breath to stop and unwind, to focus, and to de stress, for it is the best thing to focus on when we need to quiet the mind. Being aware of the breath can also help us to achieve better sleep. If we are restless or anxious then having the breath to focus certainly helps. We can learn to control the breath by breathing in and counting to four, then breathing our and counting to four. This will relieve anxiety as it slows the heart rate down and brings us back to center.

Making time to breathe

Taking time out to breathe is important for our mindfulness and we can do this during meditation as we have no other distractions around us. When we do this, we connect to the Universe and our inner being and it allows our mindfulness to shine through on a regular basis.

How to do a mindful breathing meditation

Simply lay down or find yourself in a seated position—whichever is more comfortable and keeping your spine straight to allow the energy to flow through you. Move your attention to your breath as you feel your chest and diaphragm contact and observe how it feels for the air to go in and out of your nostrils. If your mind wanders, don't worry, simply come back to your breath each time and use it as your guide.

do this for as long as you can. Fifteen minutes a day will make you more aware in your everyday life but sometimes you need to build up to that. Allow a few minutes in the day, or twice a day, to see how it makes you feel.

Simple Tips:

·During the day, if you have time, stop for one minute and focus on your breath

·When exercising, really be aware of controlling your breath as it helps to control it other times

Chapter 19: Mental Illness

Our mental well-being is just as important as our physical one, this much we now know for a fact. In a way, taking care of our mental health is similar to the way we take care of our body. We detoxify, we exercise and try to follow a healthy diet to keep our bodies in top shape. However, these are also the same things that many people tend to forget when it comes to their mental health. We hold on to negative thinking and habits that cause us to become anxious, stressed and overwhelmed on daily basis.

Mindfulness allows our mind to slow down and relax. This is how you can do it:

Connect .

Mindfulness is more than just connecting with yourself and being aware of your mind. It is also about connecting with other people and overcoming any barrier that may be hindering you from doing so. Solitude is good for the mind and body, however, too much isolation may cause you to become detached. This can lead to many negative thoughts and loneliness.

Interact with your loved ones, make new friends or go meet your old ones. Learn how to listen and be present with them. You may find that you're enjoying their company double than what you're used to.

Be Active

To keep your mind strong and more capable of being mindful, you'll need to keep fit as well. If you're feeling depressed or unmotivated because of negative thoughts, the worst thing you can do for yourself is stay stuck in a room all by yourself. If you're not ready to speak with people yet, what you can do is go out and get some exercise. Now, exercising requires a significant amount of concentration and you'll find yourself becoming more aware of every sensation, and movement you make. Focus on these things and breathe out any negative thought that might be lingering.

Keep Learning

Is exercise not your thing? Well, how about learning a new skill? This should take up all of your concentration and shift your thoughts to a more relaxed state. It doesn't matter what new activity you choose. The important thing is that you enjoy it and it keeps your attention where it's needed. A lot of people find knitting to be very relaxing whilst others prefer a more active option.

Give to Others

Be mindful of other people. Whilst mindfulness is mostly about introspection, it also teaches us to be more empathic towards the needs of others. In giving and simply providing comfort to others, we too can feel this way and absorb the positivity that radiates both ways. Volunteer at your local shelter or help out at home. Do things outside of yourself and be aware of how it makes you feel.

Start a journal.

Journals enable us to analyse our thoughts and emotions better. It also helps us understand the things that cause us stress and allow us to find the best options for dealing with them. As part of your mindfulness exercises, start a journal wherein you'll be writing all the different thoughts and feelings you've had throughout the day. Include everything, from the good and bad. Write down how you reacted to issues and what you thought about your response.

Be aware of your environment.

Look around you. Do you feel comfortable in the space you're in or is it making you feel more disconnected and anxious? If it is then don't postpone change anymore. Start small and eliminate the things that make you feel negatively. Remember, even the smallest things can influence what and how we think, so surround yourself with positivity.

Choose your activities wisely.

The things you participate in help in shaping the way your mind processes things. It can affect your perspective and of course, the way you feel. Certain lifestyle choices can be detrimental to your mental health, so be wise when choosing the kind of activities that you partake in. Just because it feels good in the moment, it doesn't mean it will be good for you in the long run. Always prioritize your well-being, physically and mentally.

Be mindful of who you surround yourself with.

Just like our environment, the people we surround ourselves with can also affect how we feel. Do you have people around you that only give off negative energy? Though it may seem cruel, it would be best if you start to limit your interaction with them until you can find a balanced ground for both of you. Explain the situation and if they really care for you, they will definitely understand.

Chapter 20: Mindfulness In Everyday Life

Mindfulness is not something that you just do at a certain time of day. You can become mindful all the time, wherever you are. You can become mindful at work, at home, while having talks with your family during dinner time, or even while watching a movie.

As you nourish and strengthen your mindfulness practice, you are making your daily experiences more special. You are breaking free from the thoughts and concerns that block your wisdom mind. You become free to cherish and experience each moment. You can truly live life to the fullest.

This chapter is about engaging your mind in mindful awareness even as you do menial, ordinary tasks. Soon, every moment of your life will be lived in mindful awareness.

Starting out your day with mindful awareness

The best way to be mindful for the day is to start with some mindfulness exercises in the morning. You can try to sit quietly for a few moments before getting out of bed. Simply sit quietly for a minute or two and feel the gentle ebb and flow of breath from your body.

You can also choose to wake up early and eat mindfully. Remember to try to bring this sense of mindfulness with you as you go about your day.

Mindfulness at work

Work is one of the biggest sources of stresses in anybody's life. A huge chunk of population even hates work because of all the stress that they have to put up with. There's stress from trying to meet a deadline, please the boss and get along with so many different people with varying work ethics.

It has even become a company's obligation to help employees relax and get along, as it has been proven that more harmony at work boosts productivity.

Mindfulness can also help you relieve a lot of that stress and tension, and give you a better and more positive work experience.

The next time that your co-workers talk to you, try to exercise patience and listen more than speak. Direct an attitude of kindness and compassion towards everyone you come in contact with. Think before you speak.

Don't be so hard on yourself because of whatever limitations you had in the past; instead, continue to move forward while learning from the mistakes you've made. This is what mindfulness is about, making meaningful connections, clearly communicating and formulating sound decisions based on actual facts rather than misconceptions.

Mindfulness at home

Although many people think that they spend a lot of time with their family, the truth is you may be there physically, but your mind is often elsewhere. Part of the attitude of thankfulness the ability to cherish every moment, experience and relationship that you have.

Be present and aware when you spend time with your family. Do away with all the random thoughts about presentations, deadlines, reports and meetings. Be thankful for your family and cherish the moments you spend with them.

Leave your work in the office. Don't take your worries and doubts home with you, and most especially, don't bring your bad mood home. Be a full-time employee at work, and a full-time father/mother/spouse at home.

Responding instead of just reacting

A reaction connotes little control over the act. It can almost be seen as automatic. You react with the first thoughts, words or actions that come to mind. On the other hand, a response can be seen as a more deeply thought out and well-considered course. Crafting a response rather than just reacting is a more responsible and positive way to go. You are actually finding ways to form a solution rather than just aggravating the situation.

When you are facing a stressful or frustrating situation at work, such as unappreciated work, misunderstandings at home or demeaning language, it becomes easy to lash out. This can lead to arguments, increased tension, and a lot of frustrated accusations flung at each other. Try to remember a similar incident happening to you. Do you think you could have handled it better? Could it have gone a different way if you had acted more rationally?

Mindful responsiveness

You can change your irrational reactions and turn them into mindful, thought out responses that can bring out the best in any situation.

The next time you are faced with just such a situation, try to go into your own head and delve into your immediate reactions with mindful patience, acceptance and curiosity. What are you feeling? Why are you feeling this way? What's the best way through this? What are your physical reactions?

As the negative emotions, thoughts and reactions spring up, catch them with mindful acceptance then let them go. Let the anger, disgust, outrage and fear pass through you with your acceptance. Accepting these feelings means you can easily let them go again. After letting all these immediate reactions flow through you, think of what the best response is. If you happen to be angry, then acknowledge your anger.

You can tell the person that you are angry and the reason why, but in a calm and controlled way. A great way to get to the root of the problem and delve deep into your own mind is to write it all down. Write a letter to the person you are angry with. Write down how you feel and why you feel that way, as well as what you would like to change and how you would prefer to be treated. You will find that writing the letter already shaves off a lot of the stress that you feel, and allow you to become clearer and more concise when expressing yourself.

Living mindfully is a great way to relieve emotional and psychological stress, not only that, physical benefits also abound. You can and will become a happier person.

Chapter 21: Find Focus And Tune Into The Here And Now

Now you're ready to move into the heart of the mindfulness meditation. You enter this phase with a concentrated focus on some object or word. This helps you clear your mind a bit from thoughts and feelings from the past or worries about the future. After you achieve this focus, you tune into what's going on where you are, in the moment.

Establish Your Focus

At this point, you've already dealt with your practical and physical needs. You've relaxed your muscles and your mind. You're breathing steadily and softly. You're ready to focus on what's happening in the present moment both within you and around you. Choose a word to say over and over as you settle into mindfulness. Use a single word or short phrase as your mantra.

Alternatively, you could to focus on an object such as a candle, figurine or if you're outside, you can focus on a tree or flower. Gaze at the object, but keep your eyes open if you want to experience the sights in your environment. Allow yourself to notice these sights, along with the sounds, smells and physical sensations you're experiencing.

The reality of mindfulness practice is that you're almost certainly going to lose focus from time to time. If this happens to you, don't sweat it. Turn your attention gently back to your focal point or word and go back to the session.

Shift into Mindfulness

Now, you can shift your attention to experiencing the here and now. Listen as a dog barks next door, a housemate slams the door or the clothes tumble in the dryer. Pay attention to the sounds and notice the way they make you feel.

Do the same thing with smells. Often, people go through life not noticing smells at all unless they're very intense or very unpleasant. Sniff the air and see what you smell. Does the room or outdoor area you're in smell fresh or dusty? Does it smell like blooming flowers, or does it smell more like rotting leaves? Notice the smells and don't judge whether they're good or bad. Just experience them as they are.

What do you see? Is the light bright or dim? Do you see any particular colors? What about people? Do you see someone coming or going in the room? Pay attention and you'll be able to describe what they're wearing accurately later on. This particular mindfulness skill is particularly helpful if you need to report a friend or loved one who has gone missing.

If you're doing a mindful eating exercise, concentrate on the sensation of taste to notice whether the food is spicy, sweet, savory or sour. If not, you can still experience the tastes of this present moment. Does your mouth taste fresh or could you really use a breath mint? Do you smell any tastes from the environment? Perhaps you're near an industrial site that brings a chemical taste to your tongue from the air. Maybe you smell car exhaust. Or, you might smell cookies baking, a fresh scent after a rain or other aromas. Notice whether these smells feel pleasant or obnoxious, but don't judge them. They aren't good or bad; they just are.

Think about your sense of touch, too. Is the floor, mat or chair you're sitting on have a distinctive texture or is it slick and smooth? Does it feel warm or cool? If you're sitting with your hands on your lap, what do your legs feel like to your fingers and what do your fingers feel like against your legs? Do you feel the slight breeze of air from a fan blowing on you or if you're outside, do you feel a stronger breeze stirring the air? Do you feel raindrops or the heat of the sun? Don't move around to feel the environment during your first sessions. Only notice what is already present in your current experience.

Pay attention to your bodily sensations. Do you feel any pain? Do you feel strength in your arms and legs or a sense of weakness? Can you feel food moving through your digestive system? Feel your heart beating. Pay attention to any skin sensations or internal rumblings. Unless you need to attend to these bodily sensations immediately, simply concentrate on the experience of feeling them.

Focus on the Here and Now

After reading the previous section, you probably understand that there's plenty to experience in this present moment. You don't need to think about anything other than what you're experiencing right now. When thoughts come up that don't have anything to do with the here and now, notice them and then let them pass like those leafs floating down the stream or like clouds moving in the sky.

Learn as Gradually as Necessary

At first, the steps leading up to (and following, to be discussed later) the mindfulness part of the sessions take longer than you'll want to or be able to spend being fully aware of the present moment, circumstances and sensations. That's okay. You'll develop your skills over time until you're spending much less time in preparation and much more time focusing on the here and now. Short mindfulness periods will gradually lead into longer ones over the course of many sessions. And remember, being mindful for a few moments at a time is far superior to never being mindful at all.

Chapter 22: Breathing Exercises Technique

Any vocalist worth their salt will value the advantages of good breath control. Building up these aptitudes enhances a vocalist's capacity to sing louder, gentler, higher, lower, with controlled tone, with more power, hold notes or expressions for more, with controlled element and expression, and in addition augmenting the wellbeing of their vocal ropes. All the fun stuff basically. Breath control is one of, if not, THE most crucial method to ace for any vocalist. Whether you are a ultra-novice, or an accomplished vocalist, you have to have a work out for your breathing muscles frequently to make strides. Great breath control originates from "wellness" of the muscles, which should be frequently practiced to be kept up.

Anyway, on the off chance that it is so awesome, why don't we all practice our breathing constantly? Alternately why are the activities we are doing not living up to expectations? These are inquiries I have regularly asked, in connection to myself and in addition my understudies. These are some conceivable answers:-

It is exhausting It's diligent work Some understudies get to be disappointed with moderate advancement Practicing inaccurately can grow unfortunate propensities Students think that it hard to discover time inside of an occupied way of life Students may think that it hard to diagram advance naturally and hence lose inspiration to do it Some understudies don't realize what to do or how to function their breathing muscles without a mentor Many understudies do not have the protection or space to practice Some understudies regularly think that it more humiliating than honing other musical abilities like playing scales on a piano for instance Some understudies may not completely welcome the advantage to singing Some understudies think that it hard to apply breathing strategies to singing tunes The propensity for some singing understudies is to practice tunes, not singing procedures.

Sort (I) not knowing how to do it. In the event that you are not certain how to inhale accurately or how to hone your system, the best strategy is to have some individual vocal instructing. On the off chance that you are now having educational cost, approach your coach to recap this for you, and give you particular guidelines of what to rehearse. Attempt this activity to get to diaphragmatic relaxing. Lie on the floor with your knees up, and feet level on the floor. Keep up the common bend of your spine, so don't squash the little of your once more into the floor. In this position, take several casual moderate full breaths. Breathe in and breathe out completely every time. Presently put a book on your lower stomach area. As you breathe in you ought to see the book rise, and as you breathe out it will lower. This is diaphragmatic relaxing. On the off chance that the book is not going up when you breathe in, you are just filling the top piece of your lungs when you relax. Focus on moving the book up as you breathe in. When you have got the hang of this, attempt to rehash this movement in a standing position, and control you breathe in by taking in for four excludes then for four checks. Build up your control by expanding the quantity of numbers. Verify you keep up complete concentrate all through to guarantee your breathing muscles are moving effectively.

In what manner would we be able to handle the second sort of hindrance - not being propelled to isn't that right?

Chapter 23: Mindfulness And Distractions

Teenagers are known for their emotional ups and downs. Life is in a constant state of flux and so by learning mindfulness, it is possible to add in a sense of peace and balance even in some small way. Mindfulness can certainly be a useful resource at their disposal.

As such, this next task builds upon the information given in the previous section and takes acceptance of the emotion, a step further looking at it through friendly curiosity.

This means that when students focus on an emotion and begin to create space, the next step is to locate the emotion and where it may be stored within the body, but to also sense all of the characteristics of the emotion. In other words, they take a friendly interest in it.

Students can imagine the emotion in a variety of colours or shapes focusing on it and imagining it as a thing of curiosity rather than a threat or a problem. This way, they recognise acceptance.

So, rather than feeling an aversion to the emotion, they have a much more creative response viewing it with barely concealed curiosity. This stops an individual from experiencing unpleasant reactions and therefore the student will not feel bad about the intensity of a negative emotion. The cycle is broken.

Thought processes

Thoughts occur in their multiples and so many are received day in and day out that it is hard to imagine gaining control over them. When you consider the sheer volume of thoughts that are experienced on a daily basis it is no surprise to imagine that they can lead to unhealthy responses or distractions.

When you consider that the human brain experiences approximately 70,000 thoughts on average in a day this means we have a different thought every 1.2 seconds.

Task:

Ask your students to imagine a time when they woke up and felt sad or despondent. They may have felt low in energy, irritable or close to tears. Sometimes for no reason. The chances are that their thoughts were gloomy too. This is because the mind immediately populates thoughts that are conditioned by the feelings experienced.

People often experience the following thoughts:

- Oh no, not again
- I don't want to feel like this
- No-one likes me
- I am so stupid etc.

These types of thoughts build on an already bad situation and can quickly escalate to gigantic proportions where negativity thrives. In many ways, a base feeling acts as a springboard to other thoughts which multiple in seconds. By teaching the students how to step back from their thoughts as well as the emotions, they will be able to realise that thoughts are just simply thatthoughts. They are not in any way a representative of reality.

Students can learn through a mindful approach to notice the thoughts that arise and to then can let go of any negativity. It's not real, they are just thoughts. They require energy from the individual to continue so when energy is withdrawn through letting go of the thoughts, this stops the feelings that arise as a result.

Students can learn to label their thoughts or simply begin to notice when their thoughts are getting the better of them and they can just remind themselves by saying the word 'thinking' to themselves just quietly. In the same way, any experience can be reduced by naming it.

It's important to note that thoughts are often inaccurate or at worst, a lie. By not always believing in the thoughts, the student can begin to feel empowered. Once they are aware of any difficult thoughts, they can accept them as natural but not helpful.

Mindfulness vs. Stress

Stress - we all experience it and learning how to manage it can be incredibly empowering. For your students, learning how mindfulness can help to manage and alleviate stress can make a big difference during their school years and certainly leading up to their exams. Importantly, by creating the foundations of mindfulness now, you are helping your students to develop vital life management skills for the future.

So why does mindfulness work in relation to stress?

☐ When a student stays in the present, they experience greater clarity of mind and optimise each experience on a moment to moment basis.

☐ When students learn the essence of mindfulness, they develop a grounding consciousness firmly based in the present and therefore, their minds are less likely to be engaged in considerations of the past or the future and, they immediately alleviate experiences or emotions that can impact their sense of well-being.

☐ When practicing regularly, students develop an enhanced ability to regulate their emotions.

☐ Students learn how to respond on a more conscious level rather than to react out of habit or through circumstance.

While pain may be inevitable in life in some shape or form, students learn that stress is optional.

For many, the way of dealing with stress is to block it out but in fact, this only increases stress levels. In mindfulness, there is an acceptance of pain on a physical and emotional level and by doing so, there is a greater ability to reduce the stress that is associated with it.

In the same way that students may struggle with their feelings and experience sensations of being powerless, helpless or feeling out of control, mindfulness can be the core resource that holds them together. It's a constant that works.

So instead of blocking the emotion or indulging in any of the following:

- ☐ Resistance
- ☐ Pushing away or denying the pain
- ☐ Clinging to the pain
- ☐ Obsessing
- ☐ Judging-negative self-talk

- If only's...
- Guilt

Mindfulness offers a sense of control through regular practice of the following techniques:

- Guided or non-guided sitting meditation
- Body scan meditation
- Walking meditation
- Yoga
- Mindful eating
- Breathing meditation
- Mindful stretching
- Mindful homework/test taking

As we have already confirmed, mindfulness practice is not all about meditation although it forms an integral part of it. Instead, practice is about a moment to moment awareness so this means that even a walk to the local shops can be mindful. Students can mindfully eat their dinner or be mindful while doing their homework.

Teenagers are distracted constantly especially when you consider that they spend most of their day using a computer, their smart phone or watching television. These days children multi-task constantly while listening to music or watching TV, by doing so, they experience increased boredom, increased sadness or unhappiness, behavioural problems and, lower grades.

Mental down-time is important for each and every individual, so, instead of the student filling every minute of every day with tasks and not taking any relevant break, instead, they take a mindful approach to their tasks, complete in a more efficient manner and then have time to relax a little.

Task:

Ask your students to write down a list of all that they have done the day before - from the moment they got up in the morning to the time they went to bed. They may be surprised to find that there was very little relaxation time. If they then look at their list and consider when they were most mindful, they may be surprised to realise that most of the time they were thinking of other things while doing those tasks.

This simple task is a great way to create awareness as to their state of mindfulness at that time. Many students will not have engaged in a mindfulness relaxation or enjoyed any meditative experience. The following task requires you to read out the meditation script below, guiding your students through the exercise (or you can obtain a guided audio meditation if you prefer) and try to encourage students to stay in the moment, avoiding any distractions.

Script:

Settle into a comfortable seated position. Disengage your mind from any busy thoughts or ideas. Close your eyes. Don't hold them shut tightly, relax the facial muscles. Gently, gather all your attention into the centre of your body. Try to contain the thoughts that take you out of yourself or serve to distract.

Let all contact with the outside world fade away.
Bring your attention to the crown of your head and then focus on every part of your body moving your focus downwards slowly.
Feel the tension in the muscles start to slip away.

Focus once more on the temple area and your forehead. Imagine that any tension stored in this area is now starting to dissolve. Imagine the tension sliding down your body and disappearing into the ground.

Do the same with your jaw, note any tension and feel it disappearing.

Focus on the neck and shoulders softening the muscles. Lift your shoulders and then gently drop them back into place imaging any tension dissipating and gradually dissolving into the ground.

Relax arms and hands imagining tension draining away.
Focus on the muscles of the back and the

spine.

Imagine knots of tension unravelling like a ball of wool. The tension will release and drift away.

Now place your mind on these areas of tension and allow the knots to unravel as you focus on them and as you do so, any tension starts to dissipate. Bring your attention to the front of your body, the chest area and stomach. Imagine your concentration – as a beam of light and as soon as the light hits any area, tension and stress dissipates.

Now turn your focus to your legs, ankles and feet and let any tension dissipate, feeling it drain through the soles of the feet into the ground.

Enjoy the moment where there is no stress. Feel comfortable, happy, contented. Appreciate the feeling where there are no worries or concerns and no stress or tension.

Gradually bring the relaxation session to a close by becoming aware of your body again and then once ready, open your eyes.

Chapter 24: Tips To Take It All The Way

You now have everything you need to start a practice, but what if you hit a few snags along the way? This chapter is about some user friendly tips to help make your practice work for you.

Consider this

This section is about all the little things you need to keep in mind to have a successful practice. After all, God is in the details.

☐ Position: there are three basic positions you can take when meditating, namely lying down, sitting up on a chair or kneeling on the floor. Make sure to extend your spine as much as possible.

o   Lying down – Lie down with your feet hip-width apart and let your feet fall naturally. You can place small cushions under your neck and knees for comfort.

o   Sitting up on a chair – It is important not to slouch or lean against your chair.

Make sure that your buttocks sit a little higher than your knees so that your pelvis can naturally tilt forward. It is best if you use an old-fashioned, wooden chair or bench.

o Kneeling – this is considered to be the optimal meditation position. Because you are so close to the ground, you can become more in tune with the energies of nature and the earth and it is also the most stable position.

However, it can be more difficult as it does take more flexibility and muscle strength. Research positions before you start if you want to consider kneeling. Try basic positions such as the Easy Kneeling position and the Burmese position before moving to the lotus position.

☐ Clothing: there are no special clothes you need to wear. You just have to make sure you're clothes are comfortable and not too tight. Make sure what you wear won't distract you in any way.

☐ Location: make sure the place where you meditate can accommodate the amount of time you need to finish your practice. Avoid places in the house that have a lot of "traffic" such as the kitchen, living room and dining room. Eventually, you might want to create a special space with a meditation altar. This altar does not have to be associated with a certain faith or religion but simply hold all the items that are special to you. It can have incense, flowers, rocks you found in nature and even pictures of your inspirations.

☐ When: basically, you can meditate whenever you have spare time. The best time for morning people is an hour right after you wake up. Being refreshed can help you be more focused and still than any other time.

For those who aren't morning people, however, right after work or before bed are also good options as they can help relax you. The downside, though, is that you might already be distracted and exhausted from the events of the day. If you have the space, you can also try meditating during your lunch break if you find that any other time is not possible.

Quick Tips that can make Meditation Easier

☐ Star with the Basics: becoming too ambitious on your first try can leave you feeling overwhelmed. Try a five-minute basic meditation before you start doing a body-tuning technique just to test the waters first.

☐ Start within your comfort zone: distractions can be your worst enemy when starting out, and doing a kneeling position that leaves you numb won't help. Start in a place, position and time that are most comfortable with you. You don't have to follow the guidelines strictly if it causes pain. Be lenient and patient with yourself. If a position is painful, try a different one. Eventually, with a few stretches every day, you will be able to do even the full lotus.

☐ Distracting aches and itches: it can be hard to maintain a certain position if you know you have to stay still. Feeling little itches and aches can pop up when you still your mind. The best way to deal with this is to be fully aware of the sensation. As you explore the sensation with curiosity and acceptance, you will find these little discomforts fade away. This is why meditation is often used as therapy for those who suffer chronic pain.

Chapter 25: Beginner's Guide To Mindfulness

..As previously stated, mindfulness is the ability to be aware of your surroundings, i.e. the present internal and external moment. If you stay focused and calm at the present moment, it's easier to restore your nervous system to balance. You can apply mindfulness to various activities such as meditation, eating, exercises or normal working. To practice mindfulness, look for:

A quiet environment

Look for a secluded place in the house, outdoors or in your office where you can easily relax without interruption or any distraction.

Be comfortable

Adopt a comfortable posture, but don't lie down as this might make you fall asleep.

Ensure you sit with the spine straight, or be in lotus or cross-legged position.

Get a point of focus

This can be an object in your room, a candle, a mantra, or an imaginary scene.

Right attitude

You shouldn't care about stress or anxious thoughts that distract your mind. If any bad thought distracts you as you relax, don't fight the thoughts but get back to the point of focus.

To practice mindfulness or visualization, sit up to avoid falling asleep during the process.

•Close your eyes and allow the worries to go away.

•Visualize yourself in a glorious or calm place. Try to see a clear picture of where you are, based on what you can feel, see, hear, smell or taste.

•Choose an imagery that impresses you, only those images that work for you and not those you wish impressed you.

•Try to incorporate as many sensory details as you can, so include at least 3 of your senses.

For example, you can visualize about a dock located on a quiet lake. Here you can easily visualize the following details;

•The amazing feeling of cool water on your bare feet

•The sight of the sun setting over the distant water

•The sounds of bird singing

•A refreshing smell of pine trees

•The taste of fresh and clean air

As you walk around the dock slowly, take your time to note the colors and the textures around you. Spend a considerable amount of time on each of your senses. Appreciate the feeling and the deep relaxation you achieve as you explore the restful place. Once ready, slowly open your eyes and get back to the present.

Chapter 26: Why Is Awareness So Important?

Greater self-awareness is at the root of mindful meditation. Prior to the 1970s, self-awareness was a somewhat vague concept. At the time, psychologists Shelley Duval and Robert Wicklund defined and advanced the link between behavior and thoughts. If we could understand our thoughts, we could increase the awareness as to why we behave in a certain way. This led to further studies and the conclusion that we can monitor thoughts and feelings as they happen.

Much of our inner life lies below the surface, in the vast region of the subconscious. Our lives are governed by patterns set long ago, sometimes at birth. Perhaps the first words out of your parent's mouth when you were born was, "Here my future doctor." Growing up, much was expected of you, and your career path was clear. Good schools, perfect grades, best college, then medical school. After an appropriate period, there would be a suitable spouse, a desirable house, followed by two adorable and well-behaved children.

If this is our internal blueprint, we might never question it. We may not even be totally aware that this has been our path from birth. It's as if we've moved on a kind of automatic pilot, with us just along for the ride. If, at age 30, we drift into a state of depression, we become utterly confused. We have achieved our dream. What could possibly be wrong?

Our mind can be conditioned in many ways. With the help of mindful meditation, we can recognize a pattern of behavior. It's this awareness that allows us to take that first proactive step toward change. We are now in the driver's seat.

There are countless ways when our conditioning simply bypasses our inner self. We are someone else's creation, not a person in our own right. Our thoughts and feelings are so deeply buried, we are no longer aware of them. Except, on some level, we are aware. But our only clue may be anger, sadness, or simply, a deadening numbness. We lose interest in things that used to excite us, we deliberately sabotage relationships, because then at least we have a logical reason for feeling miserably. Maybe we turn to drink and drugs.

Self-awareness isn't a magic pill. But when we practice mindful meditation and examine new thoughts and feelings, it serves as a roadmap to different choices and opportunities.

If you want a clue as to how awareness – or the lack of it – affects behavior, look around you. Do you have a friend who is in constant financial difficulties, but spends every weekend at the mall buying more shoes and makeup? Do you have a co-worker who constantly argues with and belittles people, yet wonders why he has no friends?

The link between thoughts and behavior couldn't be clearer. People sleepwalk through life and act on sheer impulse. They are unable to control their behavior because they are not in control of their mind and feelings. Their feelings are controlling them.

Awareness Promotes Positive Attitude & Perspective

There is another reason awareness is so important if we wish to move forward. Many of us ruminate about past wrongs. Some of us even obsess about them. Anger and bitterness can take over our mind and leave little room for anything else.

At the same time, studies show that our memories can be very different from the reality. Maybe we were bullied a few times in school. What we remember is not only the bullying, but the emotions that were a part of the experience – shame, anger,

helplessness. When we recall the bullying, what we really remember are those negative feelings. This can significantly affect how we see ourselves and how we behave toward others. Maybe we are overwhelmed by shame and feel worthless, or we thrive on anger and start bullying others before they have a chance to bully us. These behaviors become ingrained habits, and we react automatically without understanding why.

Sadly, many people go through their lives chained to a script. The dialogue for these scripts can be written in childhood, and we spend our days reacting to established clues.

Growing up, were you called stupid, unattractive, or clumsy? It may be 20 or 30 years later; maybe the people who labeled you are no longer here. But, their voices still resound in your brain, whether you're consciously aware of them or not. Every time you tell yourself, "I can't do this." "Why bother?" "No one worthwhile will ever love me," your mind replays a script that determines your actions. The path you're walking now was set long ago. The band has stopped playing, but you're still dancing to the music.

As you become aware of your life's script, it may seem like a case of mistaken identity. Every fiber of your being is arguing, "But this

isn't ME!" Whatever your pattern, it has moved you further and further from your true essence. This can be a painful realization. At the same time, it can be the key to the release from a lifetime of mental bondage.

The more you engage in mindful meditation, the more you will understand the reasons for your past actions and will be able to develop a new, alternative life script. It is never too late to change. As a matter of fact, mindfulness meditation makes it easier to open our mind and accept a different, perhaps unexplored path.

With mindful meditation, you become aware of the negative dialogue that guides your behavior. The opportunity to change the life script you've been living and open doors to better, more life- affirming choices is both exciting and challenging. But it is always worth it.

There is a possibility that some of the new awareness will make you uncomfortable. We're all human. We've all behaved badly or made mistakes we would rather not think about. And here comes mindful meditation, about to make us confront behavior we'd rather forget. It can seem scary, at first.

Eliminating Bad Habits With Mindful Meditation

To quote Dr. Phil, "You can't change what you don't acknowledge." The unwanted behavior will continue until you face it. Denial is a luxury you can't afford if you want to move forward. As a matter of fact, the problem will only worsen. Know that it is never too late to change. Sometimes, it does take some courage.

The point is so critical, it bears repeating. "You can't change what you don't acknowledge." Change isn't always easy, but may be necessary to become a better version of you.

There are other forms of meditation that urge us to brush away bad thoughts, as if they were unwelcome and unpleasant intruders. What they are, in effect, saying is that you are your thoughts. You have probably felt the effect of "bad" thoughts. "I'm a bad person." You identify yourself with your thoughts. That gives one particular thought an extraordinary power. The fault with that logic is that you are not your thoughts. Perhaps you are a person who has done a bad thing, but you are not a bad person. The difference is crucial when we attempt to change.

The "bad" thought isn't the real problem. Thoughts in themselves are neutral. When we strive for greater awareness, the issue

becomes our inclination to resist accepting negative thoughts. That just makes them more powerful and prevents us from exploring them in a non-judgmental, mindful way.

When we start to label ourselves as bad or lazy, we accept that our entire essence can be defined with one word. When that happens, we act in ways to ensure that the label fits the deed. Labels become prophetic. We act badly and lazily.

Mindful meditation brings awareness to this destructive type of self-labeling. It lets us view our thoughts non-judgmentally, apart from ourselves and begin to challenge the truth of any label. Behavior is never set in stone. When you challenge your labels, your behavior will change accordingly.

Using mindfulness, the next time you think of yourself as a bad person, you can stop the thought as it happens. Tell yourself, "Here's that silly label again. This is not who I am."

Mindful meditation allows us to recognize the labels we have accepted. With non-judgmental awareness, we can act in ways that diminish the power of labels.

Chapter 27: The Sense Of Touch

Everyday things

How does the glass feel in your hand? Is it smooth? Feel every inch of the glass?

How does it feel when you turn a door knob, knock on a door or turn a latch? How does the flip of a pan feel in your grip when you're cooking?

Get lost in touching and feeling.

Bathing

Take a bath. Let the water slowly make its climb as it fills the tub. How does the water feel when you sink down and let your arms float? How does it feel when you submerge your head and your hair is floating in the water? How does the water feel when you pour it on you?

Feel the washcloth or scrubby on your skin as you use it to clean your body. How does it feel? Imagine it scrubbing away, not only dirt, but the troubles of the day and stresses that come along with it.

How do you feel after your bath?

Rain

Go and stand out in the rain on a warm day. Raise you head to sky and close your eyes. Let the drops hit your skin and roll down to the ground around you. How does it make you feel? Do you feel refreshed? Relaxed? Focus on the sensation of the droplets hitting your skin.

Don't concentrate on any other sense. Just get lost in the way it feels when the rain meets your forehead and travels downward. Now look straight ahead and take note of how it feels when it hits the crown of your head and travels down your scalp to your neck.

Try to focus on just one drop, only one. Feel it as it travels and note where it goes.

Do this for about five minutes in a light rain.

Wind

Go outside on a day with a gentle breeze. Again, close your eyes, and focus on how the breeze feels as it caresses your skin. Focus on how your skin reacts to the breeze. Does it feel good? Do you get goose pimples? Feel the way it makes your hair swirl and flip.

Don't worry about the breeze messing up your hair. You're living in the moment and focusing on how it feels to have the breeze touch you as it continues its journey.

Do this for about five minutes in a slight and gentle breeze.

Go Barefoot

Just for a few minutes each day, take your shoes and socks off and walk in the grass. Focus on the feel on the grass on the bottom of your feet. The coolness of each blade and the way it cushions the sole of your foot.

Now, stand in a dirt patch and do the same. If you're feeling adventurous, try standing in a mud puddle. Let the moist ground cushion your foot and note the way it feels as it goes between your toes.

If you live on a beach, walk barefoot on the sand. How does the sand feel as you take deliberate steps? What is the sensation you get when it slips under foot as you lift it to make another step in your journey?

Lie down

Forget you are an adult, just for a moment. Lie down in the grass. How does the grass feel on your skin as you stretch out? Relax and close your eyes. Take in how the coolness of the grass slowly wanes the longer you lie on the ground. If it is a cool day, feel how the ground is keeping the exposed parts of you cool as it clings to the air that was there before you.

Lie on the beach. Do this on a day where the sand is warm, and do not use a blanket. Feel the sand on your body. Don't worry about it sticking to you. You can always go for a swim to wash it off.

Now, note two things as you lie on the beach, being mindful. The comfort of the warm sand beneath you and the gentle breeze that is washing over you as you lie there gives your body two experiences at once. Does this contrast invigorate you? Does it relax you? Now, try a third experience.

Move closer to the water until the only thing being touched by the ocean are your feet. How do all three sensations make you feel? Relaxed? Just stay in that moment, with a clear mind for about five minutes.

Chapter 28: How To Practice Mindfulness To Ensure Best Possible Results

To ensure best possible results from the practice of mindfulness, the individual undergoing the practices and part taking in the exercise must be able to attain and master the act of Samatha. Samatha deals with the development of attention of the person undergoing the practices, such a person must be able to maintain a high level of focus. A person taking part in mindfulness exercise must be able to shun all interference and distractions to be able to deepen his peacefulness. To do this, the person must take any of the mindfulness positions that he so desires and then focus solely on his breathing, the rise and fall of his chest, the air moving through the nostrils, the movements of the diaphragm, and the air moving through the mouth. This is the focus on nature, the sky above person. The person must also be able to ascertain where the sensation is strongest, and take notice of the first sensation as he begins to inhale and exhale. Then much focus must be placed on the other sensation that takes place in the body (seeing, hearing, thoughts, images and feelings) as they arise. Then the person can begin to count breaths as he inhales and exhales from one to ten (counting the inhale and exhale separately) and continue with this process for as long as the duration of time he has chosen to meditate (It is advisable to start up with a 20minute time frame which can be increased when it has been mastered). If the person loses count by the interference of thoughts and emotions or other external factors causing distraction and interfering with the process, he must expel the distraction and restart the process of counting on and on again.

Then he can begin with counting the inhale and exhale together, starting from one to then as usual. It is expected that thoughts, images, feelings and strong bodily sensations (which may manifest in pain and itches) will arise as the focus on breathing continues, the mind will give attention to these body sensations and images but by self-control and practice, the individual must be able to notice the drifting and interference but remain focused on the breathing pattern. With dedication, attention and focus, the person will be able to effortlessly dispel the sensations and thoughts/images and return to the breathing and counting pattern and fulfilment or realization of inner peace and happiness is derived when practiced devotedly, appropriately and consistently.

Chapter 29: Letting Go Of Negativity

We all go through life's ups and downs and sometimes life's downs seem to be more than the ups. The reason for this is that human beings have a habit of living through bad times and then reliving them. They believe that by remembering bad times, they won't make the same mistake again, although by remembering them, they actually stop themselves in their tracks from moving on.

Mindfulness meditation helps practitioners to go beyond bad memories and to think in the moment, rather than looking back. If you look at the attributes of bad memories, all of these are negative:

- I was hurt
- My health was bad
- My emotional state was awful
- My ability to cope was gone

What negative people do not realise is that they are repeating these phrases over and over in their minds until their mind accepts the negative statement as fact. These negative reminders of mistakes, used as the opposite of an affirmation, mean that people stay stuck in the past and are unable to move beyond it.

In the chapter which dealt with driving, we explained how a positive outlook helps to lighten the load. If you can't overtake, pull back and enjoy the ride. If someone cuts in and makes you brake, be nice because it's an unexpected gesture and it may actually rub off on the person. A positive response to all things which are bad helps you to be mindful of your current situation or the moment that you are currently living in.

Emotional baggage is too heavy to carry through your life. There are those who hold onto it as if it's something very precious and wonder why life isn't getting any better. Being mindful of the body and mind's need to move forward, dropping emotional baggage becomes second nature. It isn't that it didn't hurt you at the time. It's just that you have decided that you are not going to let it continue to hurt you. The mind can switch very easily from negative to positive if you let it. The thoughts that you have are personal thoughts. No one else really knows what they are. If you decide to drop a negative thought in favor of a positive one, you and all the people around you will benefit from that substitution.

How do you benefit?

You become mindful that the situation which caused you grief has passed. You strengthen your mind by affirming that it has passed and you are able to face another day as a new moment, a new opportunity to grow spiritually and mentally and let go of the bad experience. You benefit because this makes you stronger and more able to live in the moment and appreciate it.

Whenever you feel something negative in your life, replace it instantly with a positive. This is a habit that mindful people adopt because they know that holding onto negative thoughts does them no good. Imagine, you have had your heart broken by your loved one. If you hold onto that bitterness and the hurt that it caused you, you take it with you into every moment that lies ahead. If you accept that it hurt and then are able to tell yourself that today is another day, you will be better able to help your own heart to heal.

People who are broken hearted tend to stay in that moment of disappointment. They share it with people and thus spread unhappy thoughts. By teaching your mind to go forward into a new moment and see it as an opportunity, you train your mind to positive thought and that's very helpful when practising mindfulness meditation.

Chapter 28: How To Meditate For Stress Relief

Breathing Meditation

Every time you are stressed, it's a usual thing for your breathing to increase. You also tend to breathe in a swallowing manner, basically from the chest. Deep breathing exercises allow you to take fuller and slower breaths that reflect your true relaxed state. What you should appreciate about breathing deeply is that you counter stress by slowing the heart rate and reduce blood pressure.

To enhance both the physical and mental wellbeing and to manage stress, practice this 3-minute exercise at any time. The breathing exercise can help you decrease feeling of anger, frustration or tension.

Let's see a few breathing exercises that help to relief stress:

The measured breath

This technique has been proven to be very effective in stress relief. Here's how you do it:

1. Choose to either sit or stand. Ensure you relax your hands and also soften your knees. Now drop your shoulders and then allow your jaw to relax.

2. At this position, breathe in slowly through the nose. Start to count from 1-4, and keep your shoulders down. Ensure that your stomach can expand as you breathe in. Try to hold your breath for a few seconds.

3. When done, slowly release your breath very smoothly, as you do a count of 1-7. Repeat this technique for about 10-15 minutes.

The Bumble Bee Breath

As the name suggests, this technique involves making some noise to calm your mind and relieve stress and anxiety. To practice this technique, following the below steps:

1. Start by relaxing your shoulders and then close your throat slightly. You should be in a position to hear your breath as you inhale.

2. With your thumbs, cover your ears and use your fingers to cover your eyes. Keep your lips lightly closed with the teeth slightly apart and your jaws relaxed. Now breathe out slowly ensuring to make a long humming sound. Your relaxation should be long and very smooth.

3. Repeat this technique about 5-10 times and then sit. Do some long and slow breaths for a few minutes and enjoy the peace.

Massage Meditation For Stress Relief

Research has shown that it works wonders to have your tense body pressed or prodded through a gentle pressure. Massage boosts the functioning of the lungs, boosts your well-being, and improves circulation of blood throughout the body. In case you cannot do a regular full-body massage, you can opt for an occasional facial, manicure, or pedicure. These massage practices can nurture and treat your trigger points to relieve stress and anxiety.

Try this 5-minute self-massage meditation technique in order to calm and relieve stress

- Begin by kneading the muscles located at the back of the neck and shoulders.

- Make a loose fist and then drum up and down the sides and the back of the neck.

- Now use the thumbs to start working out tiny circles around the base of the head or skull.

- Use your fingertips to slow massage the rest of the scalp. Tap the fingers against the scalp and move them from front to back, and later over the sides.

- Start to massage the face. Make a series of little circles using the fingertips or the thumbs. Pay attention to the jaw muscles, forehead, and the temples.

- Massage the bridge of your nose using the middle fingers, and progress to work outward on the eyebrows and temples.

- Now close your eyes and cup your hand loosely over your face. Inhale and exhale easily for a moment.

To make the massage more productive, incorporate massage oils such as almond essential oil.

Walking Meditation

Walking is a very effective way to relieve stress as it puts your mind in a meditative mood, especially when walking in a green area or park. In addition to stress reduction, walking helps you to lose weight, feel lighter and allow you to exercise more. Here are a few steps to effectively meditate when walking to reduce stress and achieve pure consciousness:

- Choose to walk in a quiet place such as around a lake or a park.

- As you walk, do not rush, just take it easy, making your strides as short as possible.

- Focus on your senses in order to forget about the anxious thoughts such as the smells, sights, or sounds of nature.

- Take some deep breaths to relieve tension from your head down to your feet. Continue with a few breaths without getting distracted. Try to have your earphones or headphones on in case you cannot concentrate as soothing background music can work wonders.

Chapter 29: Mindfulness For Working Professional

Every working professional who practise mindfulness must realize that to achieve good performance and for stress reduction at their workplace, there is a need to practise mindfulness at a daily basis. This is a good way to cope with ever increasing stress due to the demanding work schedules and higher goals of the organisation.

There is often a need for an individual to build better capability to accomplish more in life and this may achieve through a deliberate attempt by individuals to enhance their mental strength of handling stress. Reflection and meditation are very effective methods for any working professionals in aid to reduce stress at an extreme pressurising workplace. As relief obtained from reflective thinking, the capacity of the mind to handle stressful events will also increase and eventually lead to elevating of self-confidence and improving performance at work.

HOW IT WORKS

The human nature is more incline to focus on negative experience than positive experience and subconsciously the mind will keep play back any unpleasant memories whenever similar situation occurred. Even though the mind is doing its job to protect and warn you of any dangers, yet it may not benefit you if you constantly living in the past or fear of the future. Mindfulness allow you to take control of your thoughts and feelings, and differential between those NOW thoughts (present-orientation) and other thoughts (past or future-orientation), that will help you to obtain calmness and confidence in facing current challenges and being effective in problem-solving.

The purpose of mindfulness is to let you be aware of your feelings and thoughts, labelled them in a realistic manner, with a non-judgemental attitude and living in the NOW moment so that you will not be burn-out, stressed-out and discouraged easily at any time.

Mindfulness practice enable you to take a position as a third party viewing the situation, such as watching cars go by the road in front of your house or watching birds filed by the sky above your head. Thoughts and feelings come and go, but we need to learn to let go of those unhealthy thoughts and feelings which hinder us to move on in life. Nevertheless, our thoughts and feelings do not define who we are and what we want, for they are a process that aid us to make a right choice whenever we need to presently.

If a bothering thought comes to your mind and you feel anxious, you may want to label the feeling: "This feeling is anxiety", and to identify the thought which arose the anxiety: "This thought is bothering me". As you let the feeling go and give your attention to your present moment, you may begin to feel better and will be more open for any opportunities in the horizon. Indulging in a bothering thought may set a smaller boundary to your desirable outcomes, so be mindful of your thoughts, for there are still many people out there who do not make any effort to respond appropriately to their thoughts.

When you are not mindful of those thoughts and feelings you harbour within your mind, your future experience would be limited. Before diving into how mindfulness works, let us understand the relationship between your thoughts and feelings.

Conclusion

Much of the content of the book is easily transferrable into numerous activities and hobbies. I am pretty sure anyone engaging in pottery and using a potters wheel appreciates how they must remain in the moment, or face a big mess as their clay misshapes and goes everywhere.

The content can be applied to any sport and the examples given are merely that. I am sure you would notice how easy it is to consider how these approaches can be used with weight lifting, cycling, rowing. How they can be used when doing homework or writing a book.

As you incorporate moments of mindfulness into your day, it can become easier to increase the number and the duration of those moments. Until, maybe, one day, you'll notice that thoughts that once bothered you, now wash over you a little easier.

It is never the purpose of mindfulness to change our experience, it is just one of the best side effects of mindful engagement with life.

I do hope you have enjoyed this brief text, and you put into practice at least one thing from within these pages. My sign of a useful course, workshop, or book, is that I get at least one useful idea or skill from engaging with the content. I also hope that you found this text an ideal length as I am aware that too many books recycle too much content. I am not a fan of filler material and strive to keep that out of anything I write.

www.ingramcontent.com/pod-product-compliance
Lightning Source LLC
Chambersburg PA
CBHW072009070526
44583CB00015B/1404